Coles to Jerusalem

A pilgrimage to the Holy Land
with the Reverend Richard Coles

PALLAS ATHENE

Foreword

The custom of making a pilgrimage, once common in these islands, is now practiced by a marginal few, and most of them Muslims rather than Christians. It is 'mini-breaks' that most people long for now, to which we are so accustomed that there was a slight awkwardness about the group that gathered at Heathrow for our pilgrimage to the Holy Land. For most it was the first time and perhaps they felt it would be wrong to stop at the Champagne Bar or go mad in Duty Free following in the footsteps of Our Lord (or my Lord).

Fortunately any sense of solemnity soon wore off as we discovered, or rediscovered, that a pilgrimage requires no particular preparation or attitude of mind. It has its own dynamics and by day two these pilgrims, consciously or not, were conforming. Conforming to what? To the narrative of the life and death of Jesus of Nazareth, the itinerant preacher from green Galilee, who was baptised by John in the Jordan, and got into trouble with the Jerusalem authorities who put him to death.

This much we know with a fair degree of certainty. The greater claims for Jesus the Christ are a matter of faith. Even so, the story is so powerful, and the sheer volume of people trying to follow it so impressive, that even those untroubled by metaphysical speculation are drawn in to a collective experience.

How fascinating to have a writer on board, not only participating, but observing and recording it with the explicit aim of working up our trip. Some were not entirely comfortable about this, so Kevin allowed us to see and correct and point out anything we did not agree with or like; reading his first and then final draft added another degree of interest. I, naturally, went to considerable trouble to conceal my venal nature and was either successful, which I doubt, unwitting, which is likely, or even more likely a beneficiary of Kevin's charitable nature.

It is fascinating too to read an account of a pilgrimage written by someone who would not, I think, describe himself as a card-carrying member of the club. But events in bars, late night conversations, the social dynamics of a settling group, were no less absorbing for those following an explicitly religious itinerary than for those who weren't – and if that ever lapsed into abandon and frivolity, which fortunately it did most nights, the sober reality of life today in Israel/Palestine was never far away.

For me as a priest and an aspiring follower of Christ what holds these together is the people and places from the New Testament narrative: Sychar, where a notorious woman meets Jesus at the well; the pool at Bethesda, where a paralyzed man trampled in the rush finally is healed; Emmaus, where the disciples, devastated by Jesus' arrest, trial and execution, suddenly realize a stranger beside them on the road is Him, unbelievably living again.

For me, the end of our journey reaches the same point as theirs; when we look at the person beside us and see, unbelievably, Jesus living.

The Reverend Richard Coles
Autumn 2016

From London to Galilee

Than longen folk to goon on pilgrimages.
Chaucer, General Prologue to the Canterbury Tales

INTRODUCING FATHER RICHARD

Let me begin by telling you a little about my good friend Richard Coles, better known as the Reverend Richard Coles, who cares for the souls of his parishioners in Finedon, a small Northamptonshire village. Father Richard, whose spectacles sometimes lend him an owlish look (he is indeed a scholar) and whose features can appear rather stern at times (he is anything but), is possessed of a personal charm so powerful that I sometimes think of it as a weapon. I have seen him beguile the most irate and aggressive strangers with a few soft sentences. The members of his flock obviously adore him, as well they might. ("Adore" is a very Richard word. It pops up every four or five pages in his memoir *Fathomless Riches*.)

Richard is wonderful company, and is full of paradoxes. These days, he is modest and self-effacing to a fault, yet he still loves showing off, as he freely admits. His faith, which came to him quite late in life after many godless, rackety years, is profound, but he knows how to carry it with lightness and grace in our messy, workaday and predominantly secular word. He knows, as all true Christians should, that he is a sinner, but he also knows that his Redeemer liveth. Quite a few people have told me how he has committed many small but valuable acts of kindness and generosity, keeping his charity private.

Richard laughs loudly at his own frequent quips and even more loudly at others'. He likes to divert himself and his companions of the day with unexpected questions ("What type of restaurant would you most like to own?"), daydreams ("I wish I lived in a hotel and could have my laundry washed and ironed every day – proper linen sheets…") and thought-experiments ("If you could invite six people from any point in history to your dinner party, who would they be?"). He is given to saying things like: "I love being a priest. People are always giving you things, and you can dress up all the time."

If you live in the United Kingdom, you will almost certainly have heard and seen Father Richard on BBC radio and television. He's been involved in various kinds of broadcasting for a couple of decades, and is probably best known as the co-presenter of BBC Radio 4's light-hearted morning chat show Saturday Live, which has about two million regular listeners. Richard has a beautiful radio voice: quiet but distinct, just a little bit on the posh side – Richard is indeed a little bit posh – and so

soothing that he should really be given a late-night slot
to beguile insomniacs into sweet sleep.

He is an excellent radio interviewer for the same
reason that he is a fine priest: he knows how to listen
with just the right mixture of sympathy and insight.
He is also very quick-witted, and once in a while rather
cutting. I recall once almost choking with laughter
when I heard him presenting a late-night Radio 3 programme in which he was to have been joined by
Richard Dawkins, the noted atheist and enemy of religious superstition. "We're sorry to say that Richard
Dawkins has just called us to say that he won't be joining us after all." Slight pause. Then, throwaway: "Typical Aries."

On television, he is noted for his self-effacing but
laser-sharp contributions to comedy quiz shows such
as QI, Have I Got News For You and Pointless. (He
posted a picture on Facebook showing his green room
for the last: "Rev Richard Coles: Pointless." He does
not, you will gather, take himself too seriously.) Early
in 2014, he won the Celebrity Mastermind competition – a feat which came as no surprise at all to anyone
who has ever spoken with him. Richard carries a hefty
erudition, though he is careful to deploy it gently. His
special subject on the quiz was the series of genteel and
malicious Mapp and Lucia novels by E. F. Benson.
This, too, was no surprise to his friends.

Now, if you knew that much already, you probably

also know that Richard was once famous for entirely different accomplishments. He was a pop star. A proper, chart-topping, wild-living, drug-taking, mobbed-by-fans pop star.

In the 1980s, Richard was a keyboard player for The Communards, an outfit that stood out of the general run of eighties beat combos because of (a) their radical politics – the Communards took their name from the Paris Commune, and played any number of benefit gigs for causes dear to the Left; (b) the unique and unforgettable high-pitched vocal style of their diminutive lead singer Jimmy Somerville; (c) the fact that he and Mr. Somerville were both Out and Proud; and (d) their knack for recycling classic African-American soul music into club anthems for the second great disco era. Their biggest hit, "Don't Leave Me This Way", was also the top-selling single of 1986 in the British charts. Richard made a lot of money very rapidly, and, like many another young star, lost most of it almost as rapidly. He appears on television not only for the fun of the thing but with an eye to keeping his pension topped up.

Just as well, then, that Richard is now the British media's favourite clergyman, so much so that he is in severe risk of becoming a National Treasure.

When he moved to Finedon a few years ago, a handful of local Anglicans deserted the church, because they did not like the idea of their minister being openly gay. The members of this small, indignant group proved to be very much out of step with local opinion. Attendances at Richard's church have, I'm told, all but doubled, and his flock are both fond and proud of Richard and his life partner David – a slim, handsome fellow with a natty beard, who is also a clergyman, and who shares the Finedon vicarage. Father Richard and Father David dote on their four dachshunds: Horatio, Audrey, Daisy Mumu and Willie Pongo.

I first met Richard at BBC Broadcasting House, near Oxford Street in the heart of London, some time back in the mid nineties or so. En route to theological studies and then ordination, Richard had an interim career as a more or less full-time broadcaster; among other roles, he was one of the main presenters on BBC Radio Three's live highbrow arts-and-ideas programme Night Waves, to which I was an occasional contributor. It was soon clear to me that Richard's diffident, sympathetic manner was the public face of a keen intellect. I liked him very much, and at once. (We didn't see each other much during his transitional years from the BBC to the C of E, but we had the occasional lunch and now, thanks to the rise of Facebook, are in touch almost daily. One of Richard's gifts to his Facebook posse is a regular mini-essay on the saint of each passing day, beautifully written and full of delightfully improbable facts.)

Forward to a Friday afternoon in the early autumn of 2013. Richard and I have found out that we are both

going to be in studio at BH for our respective pro-
grammes – Saturday Live and Saturday Review – and
we agree to meet for a coffee at about five. Naturally,
this plan develops mission creep, and we end up at the
George, a pub much haunted by BBC staff over the
years. According to some biographers, it is the original
of the Chestnut Tree in Orwell's 1984, the boozer
where, at the bitter end of the novel, Winston Smith
capitulates to Big Brother while drinking Victory Gin.
BBC musicians used to call it The Gluepot, because
they found it so difficult to raise themselves out of their
seats once a proper drinking session had begun. We talk
of many things, including our hopes and schemes and
projected travels for the year ahead.

"I'm taking a group of my parishioners on a pilgrimage to the Holy Land in March", said Richard.

"Really? That sounds fascinating. I wish I could
come…"

"Why don't you?"

Pause.

"…. I'm not a parishioner."

"That doesn't matter."

Pause.

"I'm not a Christian. Not even an Anglican. I'm
probably an atheist, really. Though I seem to recall that
I was christened as a child…"

"That's still all right. Come."

So I came.

DAY ONE: MONDAY 17 MARCH
LONDON TO THE SEA OF GALILEE

We gather early-ish, just before 8.00 am, at the Heathrow Airport departure lounge, some 25 of us. About half of the party is made up of Richard's Finedon parishioners; the other dozen or so already know each other, at least slightly, from a briefing session held at the Vicarage a couple of weeks ago. I am the only one who has met no-one here except the Reverend Coles. It feels slightly awkward – like being a schoolboy tagging along on another school's field trip. Do they know I am planning to write about them? (They do.) Do they know I am not a Christian? (They soon will.) Will they be angry or troubled when they find out? (Not at all.)

Father Richard and Father David – who I now meet for the first time – are both wearing clerical black and dog collars. But the Finedon pilgrims bear nothing to distinguish them from the other passengers this morning; no badges, no Bibles, no obvious religious emblems apart from the odd small, discreet crucifix on a chain. "We" – I am already starting to think of us in the first person plural – are mostly Middle-Englanders, mostly middle-aged or a little older, mostly carrying beach-type novels or newspapers and cardboard cups of coffee. None of us would dream of asking other passengers if they had Accepted Jesus as Their Personal Saviour (the chilling words with which I was once greeted by an elderly American pastor at the start of a thirteen-hour trip to Colorado). We are, to use a very English word, "Nice". If you, too, are nice, you would probably like us.

Richard introduces me to a couple of the new faces. One of them is John Patrick Devlin – "J. P." – who is one of the regular contributors to the Saturday Live show. J. P. is an average-sized chap with a semi-permanent smile, a shining pate and a strong Belfast accent. Strictly speaking he is a Roman Catholic, born and raised, but he quietly confides to me that he no longer really believes in the supernatural side of the faith. He and I are probably the only non-believers on the trip.

On the British Airways flight I sit alone and try to concentrate on a short book about the Palestinian-Israeli conflict. (About which I will not be writing much here, except when its signs and scars are impossible to ignore.) It's a clear and, as far as I can judge, reasonably balanced account of the whole horrible and agonising mess, but I find it hard to wrap my head around the subject. It deepens my resolve to look and listen about the politics of the region rather than to talk from a position of ignorance. After an hour or so I am so depressed that I give up and read my novel instead. Then I fall asleep.

✠ ✠ ✠

Five hours after take off, we arrive at Tel Aviv airport. As a certified religious tour party, signed up with a long-established local company specialising in pilgrimages – the aptly named Shepherd's Tours – we have an easy time passing quickly through the airport's famously strict Security and Passport Controls, and on to meet our coach. We'll be spending a lot of time on coaches over the next ten days. It's early evening and the air is warm, but not oppressively so.

Rami, who will be our tour guide, is a Palestinian Christian, from Bethlehem. He was born in 1979, and is married, with two small children. He's wiry – slender, short-haired, fashionably dressed in tight jeans and tight sweaters. He favours what appear to be designer-label sunglasses and a fancy watch, and he smokes with enthusiasm whenever he spots an opportunity. There is something of a swagger to him, suggestive of a successful football player, or possibly a successful dealer. Throughout the trip, he is constantly being interrupted by the ring-tone of his mobile phone, and is often caught up in intense conversations. At a guess, he has lots of other commercial irons in the fire, or a highly active social life. Probably both.

Rami has the traditional tourist-guide's gift of the gab, expressing himself in idiosyncratic but fluent, extremely rapid English, and he clearly knows a great deal about the history of the Holy Land and its peoples, though I wonder how much of his account would pass muster with historians. His public sense of humour tends to the harmless and corny – usually little gags about needing to be paid to pose for photos, or threatening to impose fines on us for naughty behaviour. But his extraversion doesn't entirely conceal some darker emotions, not far from the surface – what might be sadness, and what might be anger or worse. Probably best not to wonder, just yet, what hostilities and resentments might lurk behind his professional friendliness. He'll make a few of them clear enough over the next few days.

Father Richard, seated at the front of the coach, picks up a microphone and explains that our itinerary for the pilgrimage is designed (with just a couple of minor digressions) to follow the narrative of Christ's life, from Galilee and Nazareth to Jerusalem and Calvary. Then Richard hands the mike back over to Rami, who spends the next hour or so giving us a crash course in this country's history, from Alexander the Great to now.

Most people read, doze, or stare out at the scenery, which for this first part of the journey is unremarkable, and might be almost anywhere on the Mediterranean. Trying to be a good reporter, I make notes on his talk. When I read them later, they are largely incomprehensible:

> Samaritans. Hellenistic blood [?] 5,000 soldiers murdered [?] Pompey. Herod: 44-28 BC. Ruler. Civil War in 28 BC. There have been three

"famous" Herods. Pontius Pilate. Destruction of the Second Temple. Persian Invasion. Islamic Invasion. First Crusade. 55,000 Crusaders. 1297 Crusaders leave. Saladin. Mameluk rule. "Tough time for us." 1517 - 1917: Ottoman Empire. Exactly 400 years of Occupation. Cut off from Industrial Revolution. British mandate was from 1917 to 1947. "Good news for Christians!" – except that Muslims believe that Christians are conspiring with the British. Jewish state 1947. Ceasefire till 1967. 1979 Peace agreement. [Ravi calls it a "Big Lie"…] Arafat. Cutting supplies to PLO. 1987 – first Intifada. "Economic" Intifada. Oslo agreements. Suicide bombers. Death of Arafat…

The sun is completely down by the time we reach our destination: the Pilgerhaus Tabgha, a German-run hostel for Christians journeying to the Sea of Galilee. It has been here in one version or another since 1889; today, it is a spacious hotel built in a kind of diluted Bauhaus style with large public meeting places. It's set in lush, fragrant gardens, with a good view of the nearby lake. A clean, well-lighted place, but with a touch of asceticism about it, as if too many domestic comforts would compromise its earnestness.

After unloading our bags, collecting our keys and finding our rooms (to my relief I do not have to share with anyone), Richard summons us to a gathering in the chapel – not a service, just a briefing. Richard asks us to introduce ourselves with a few sentences each. Time to start putting at least a few names to faces; never one of my strong suits. Over the coming days, these will grow into the names of new friends: Mo and Bryan, Trudie, Helen, Erica, Nicholas… Richard says a few impromptu words about pilgrimages in general and the Islamic concept of hajj in particular. I wander back to my room, and, full of good intentions, pick up my copy of the New Testament. (King James Version; I am one of those insufferable atheists who is a literary snob about more recent translations. I should be ashamed of myself. But the Biblical passages we will be using for all our services here come from the New Revised Standard version, copyright 1989.) Within seconds I am asleep. I snooze on through the time when I am meant to be joining the pilgrims for Evensong, and only wake up in time for our first shared meal in the brightly lit refectory. The food, a help-yourself dinner, is healthy and adequately tasty, but the true relief for those of us partial to a spot of liquid refreshment is that you can buy beer and wine! Not cheap, but perfectly potable.

I look around for the friendliest face and decide to sit down next to Nicholas, a tall, sturdily built, gregarious chap from Manchester, late thirties or so, with close-cropped hair and a ready grin. Nicholas, who works as a librarian, is definitely the loquacious type, with a nice line in self-deprecating humour. I like him at once; it would be hard not to. Nicholas introduces me to his friend Colin, Glaswegian by origin, Mancunian by election. Colin used to be in the Territorial Army, a fact that is easy to credit as he is stocky, heavily muscled and, to be frank, looks like the kind of thug you would least like to meet down a dark alley. Like many a strong man, Colin is in reality as gentle and sweet-natured as... well, as Nicholas. This is reassuring. Even if I don't hit it off with anyone else, these two will be good, down-to-earth company. It gradually dawns on me that they are probably a couple, but I decide to let them make the first mention.

Dinner over, we sit outside. The air is still warm enough for shirt-sleeves, but pleasantly fresh. Today is the birthday of Helen, a proud Yorkshire woman who is, at least to my inexpert eye, the most exquisitely dressed and impeccably groomed of us all. (Not that she has much sartorial competition. The Fathers dress and overheat in their clericals during the day, but the rest of us favour loose and comfortable leisure wear. Only Erica, a best-selling novelist whose latest book is in the Sunday Times top ten this week, dresses as tastefully as Helen.)

Helen used to be a fashion model, both on the catwalk and for magazines, and then she went on to found her own successful business. She is very funny, and likes to tease other people on their little pomposities. She also likes to pretend that she's the kind of no-nonsense

Northern lass who reads nothing more intellectually challenging than *Vogue* – a mask that fools no one, and anyway begins to slip over the next few days when she blurts out inadvertent comments on such topics as Romanesque architecture, Handel, the minor painters of the Italian Renaissance and the design of jet propulsion engines.

Most of the party have wisely opted for early nights, but for the few of us left on the patio it seems rude not to sit up till the witching hour for a nightcap. Or two. Some aspects of this pilgrimage might not be too arduous after all.

DAY TWO: TUESDAY 18 MARCH

The sun is already bright and the day promises to be warm. We gather in the car park to board or coach. Rami is already here, and before we set up, he asks each of us to choose a "buddy" for the duration of the pilgrimage. Every time we re-board a coach, Rami will call out "Buddy Check", and we each have to spot our partner. This simple trick, it seems, is a great help in making sure that absent-minded wanderers are not unwittingly left behind. My Buddy for the duration will be Sara, a well-known and distinguished writer and theologian, whose last major book was about the spiritual strength to be found in the solitary life. (I later overhear one of the pilgrims referring to her as "a wonderful hermit from Scotland".) She is short and slight, and on bright days like these keeps her long mane of wild grey hair covered by a big floppy hat. She is a smoker of quite heroic determination.

Rami hands us out ear-pieces; today, and for most of our trips, he will give his commentaries by murmuring into a small microphone, so as not to disturb other groups. We embark, and sit back to admire the scenery. The first surprise: Galilee is green, fresh and fertile, not at all the parched and unforgiving semi-desert that we tend to picture if our Biblical education never went very much past Sunday School level. The deserts and the wilderness are in the south of the country; but this is a fat and pleasant land. Jesus spent his childhood and youth among olive trees and streams, nearby the giant lake we call the Sea of Galilee. He did not encounter the waste lands until he left his home in adulthood and set off for His mission. Rami begins his commentary by telling stories about the Crusades. He pronounces the familiar "Saladin" in the unfamiliar (but obviously accurate) Arabic version – it sounds like Salad-ahin.

Even in the mundane context of a coach trip, touches of wonder start to bubble to the surface of the mind. At one point Rami refers to "pig-shepherds", and we realise that we are gazing across at the place where Christ cast out demons, and sent them into the bodies of the Gadarene swine. Trudie later points out to me that there is an unspoken political element to this Biblical references: the "pig-shepherds" were not Jewish, and yet they had a right to their land. An important point for a Palestinian Christian.

Cattle wander freely, grazing on leaves and shoots and lush grasses. We pass by olive grove after olive grove – the region is noted for the excellence of its oil. A road sign reads: "Nazareth 31 km", and I feel my scalp prickle just a little. This type of fertile scenery, Rami suggests, is what the Scriptures wish to evoke in the phrase "Land of milk and honey".

It is, to be a sure, a Paradise bristling with modern serpents. Rami points at a sprawling compound which is, he says a "Five-Star Prison", where rich prisoners – politicians found guilty of corruption and the like – work out their sentences in comfort. He also points to an IDF military base, on our left. It is crammed with missiles.

By way of a spontaneous pop quiz, Richard asks us if we can remember any episode in the New Testament in which it rains. We are all stumped, though the question launches an interesting set of digressions on the role of rain in English literature: *King Lear*, *The Tempest* and so on. Since I have been thinking, for obvious reasons, about Chaucer's *Canterbury Tales* for the past few days, I suggest that you could say that Eng. Lit. actually begins with a couplet about the rain:

Whan that Aprille with his shoores soote
The droghte of March hath perced to the roote...

Not strictly true, of course, but poetry usually trumps pedantry. Talk of rain and the growth of plants leads Richard to the first of his several musings on the theme of pomegranates.

The pomegranate, Richard tells us, is bursting with spiritual symbolism. First there is the folklore about pomegranates and the Jewish law: the number of seeds in each fruit is said to be identical to the number of Mosaic laws. The fruit is also a symbol of resurrection in both Christianity and Islam, which is why it is an important carved motif in the Alhambra, Granada. He recommends that when we reach Jerusalem, we might want to buy ceramic pomegranates at the well-known Armenian pottery near our hotel. And the conversation drifts on to that strange and beautiful Armenian film, *The Colour of Pomegranates*...

Cana

Richard's talk may have been a subtle kind of sales pitch, as the first thing we encounter as we walk up the steep hill into Cana is a souvenir shop offering sample glasses of the local pomegranate wine. It tastes a little like sweet port gone slightly to vinegar, with strong fruit notes. An acquired taste, no doubt, but one which none of us plans to acquire. The place is stuffed from floor to ceiling with pious artefacts; alas, most of them are pure kitsch to our eyes, and not many sales are made.

Cana in Galilee, to give it the full name, is the site of Jesus' first miracle: turning water into wine.

> And the third day there was a marriage in Cana of Galilee and the mother of Jesus was there: and both Jesus was called, and his disciples, to the marriage. And when they wanted wine, the mother of Jesus saith unto him, They have no wine...   [John 2:1-3]

The church at Cana is, for obvious reasons, a popular place to hold weddings nowadays. As we arrive a wedding seems to be in progress... but something about it seems a bit fake – as Trudie sneers, a bit "Disney-fied". The moderately handsome groom and his much more attractive bride have no family or friends waiting on them, only a photographer. Clearly some kind of photoshoot, probably possibly for a fashion magazine, or a specialist publication for Brides-to-Be.

Here, we have the first of the many short services: a reading from John 1:1-11, and a short modern hymn, "Come, join in Cana's feast..." Our service takes place in the:

Church of the Annunciation

According to the Greek Orthodox tradition, this occupies the site in which the Angel Gabriel came to tell Mary that she was to give birth to the Son of God. More certainly, the Church was built on this site by the Crusaders, and one of its main functions was to protect their water supplies from the enemy. Today, the Church is run by Franciscans. We gather for a brief service, and have only just completed when the monks come along to shoo us away as it is almost noon. Trudie compares the experience to "closing time at the Queen Vic", which I think must be an allusion to a pub in some soap opera. In more scholarly vein, she points out that the noise of the Angelus we can now hear is coinciding precisely with the adhan – the muezzin's call to prayer.

It is tempting to linger here and look out from our high vantage point across the landscape. But we have a timetable to obey.

Nazareth

The next stop is Nazareth, a busy, modern town in which cars race by at a frightening rate or back up into noisy jams, where the streets overflow with pedestrians, not rude exactly, but not that chummy either. It is noisy, dusty and, to be frank, none too pretty.

Rami begins his commentary with the interesting observation that in the time of Christ, Nazareth was a kind of dormitory town: men came used it more as a base for travelling out to follow their trades and skills than as a place to make a home. So Joseph, father of Jesus, may have been unusual in choosing to settle here.

Our first stop is a small building, formerly a synagogue, now a place for Christian worship: the Synagogue Church of Nazareth. Here, the reading is from Luke 4:14-21. It tells of how Jesus went from town to town in Galilee, until he returned to his home town of Nazareth and, one Sabbath, followed tradition by reading aloud from the text handed to him – the book of the prophet "Esaias" [Isaiah]. Christ reads:

> The Spirit of the Lord is upon me,
> Because he hath anointed me to preach the gospel
>   to the poor;
> He hath sent me to heal the broken-hearted, to
>   preach deliverance to the captives,
> And recovering of sight to the blind,
> To set at liberty them that are bruised,
> To preach the acceptable year of the Lord.

Jesus closes the book, and sits down. Everyone is startled, and gazes at him in silence. Then he says a shocking thing:

> This day is this scripture fulfilled in your ears.

He has declared himself.

The Church of St Joseph

This is built on the site believed to have been the house of Joseph. Can it be true? If so, everything here suggests that Joseph was very far from being the humble horny-handed son of toil we know from the picture books of our childhood, but a solidly prosperous businessman and property owner.

Rami offers his explanations and commentaries. According to him, the carpenters of New Testament times were in fact all-purpose craftsmen who played an important role in building construction, and were well paid for their efforts. Joseph would, if the comparison is acceptable, be more like a well-established member of the Nazarene upper middle classes: a man of substance and the owner of an impressively large dwelling.

The cellar beneath the church is held to be Joseph's "house" – really a large, modified cave; Fred Flintstone would have felt at home here. As you weave and crouch through its passages, you can see the remains of a large oven; a ritual purification pool, where acts of religious cleaning would be held twice a day, at sunrise and sunset; an escape tunnel with an entrance that could readily be sealed against attackers; and an area where the livestock can be tethered: "Donkeys, not camels," Rami insists. According to Rami, Joseph would have been well advanced in years when he built this sizeable dwelling – around 50 to 55. His young wife Mary would have been about 14 or 15.

Back out into the sun, the noise and the crowds. On the way back down the hill, an accordion player strikes up with "When The Saints Go Marching In". Some of us sing and strut along; a faint but distinct sense of community is beginning to stir among us. At the bottom of the hill, Richard points out a huge poster that glares down from a hoarding at the bottom of the hill. It warns Christians, in the sternest terms and in several languages, against the blasphemy of treating "Issa" (Jesus) as God rather than a prophet.

I scribble in my notebook: "Hard to retain a sense of the numinous in such a noisy, traffic-crammed modern town."

We have lunch at a religious school, and then head back to Galilee.

We are back at the hostel before five. I decide to be a good student and spend a couple of quiet hours reading the Gospel according to Luke, and a long essay about the New Testament by an Oxford theologian, John Drury. It is unexpectedly wide-ranging. I scribble notes and questions next to the names of poets and philosophers mention by Dr Drury: Coleridge and Tennyson, Locke and Spinoza… It is partly daunting, partly dismaying. By seven, feeling something akin to mental indigestion, I head down for dinner, hungry not so much for food as for talk and laughter. Fortunately, these are plentiful.

I chat to Nicholas and Colin again; they have clearly decided that I am not a bigot, and so we ramble on about matters gay as well as on librarianship, on the good and bad aspects of Manchester and on Nicholas's religious studies as a mature student. A very touching moment comes when Nicholas tells me that as a teenager, sure of his sexuality but unsure of where he stood in theological terms, he worried for a long time that "Jesus might not love me because I was a gay person." The thought of cheery Nicholas racked by these spiritual doubts almost makes me want to weep. Drawing on my few scraps of New Testament learning, I ask (a) is it not the case that one of Christ's big things was that it's up to us to try to love each other?, and (b) is it not that case that Christ's references to homosexuality add up to precisely zero? Nicholas and Colin nod. They're over and done with that kind of angst. But they do admit that they would have thought twice about coming on a pilgrimage led by, shall we say, a more traditional vicar than Richard.

Meanwhile, other pilgrims, more energetic and enterprising, go for a long walk by the Sea. They come back with tales of animal sightings – a friendly donkey, and a family of rock badgers.

DAY THREE: WEDNESDAY 19 MARCH

A very short coach trip takes us down to the edge of the Sea of Galilee, where Father Richard and Father David will conduct a mass in the open air. They are both dressed in white robes, with (I have to ask the proper word) bright yellow stoles draped over their shoulders. As they carefully prepare an altar on top of a large, flat stone, we chat quietly, or simply look around us at the water and the hills. How strange and dream-like to be at the edge of a lake whose name we have known since earliest childhood.

A handsome young German priest, a Catholic with the apt name of Christian, comes to join us. He is softly spoken, and smiles gravely as he admits that, strictly speaking, he is "not allowed to commune" with us. He pauses. "But… the Church in Rome is far…" Gentle laughter. We won't be telling on him.

This is the first full-scale service we have held, and before we begin, Father Richard asks us each to compose a small prayer. One by one we read them out loud. Some are prayers for the sick and the dying, some for the dead (one of our number has been left a widow in the last year, and is still raw with mourning), some for our hopes for the pilgrimage itself. A man and a woman are both in tears. When it comes to my turn, I read out: "I am very grateful to be part of this company, and I hope everyone here will find what I have already found." Meaning, I suppose: a comfortable sense of having been accepted and even welcomed, despite everyone being aware by now of my awkward and ambiguous status on the journey.

After the service is done, Rami asks us a question about the Gospel of John, 21:11

> Simon Peter went up, and drew the net to land full of great fishes, an hundred and fifty and three: and for all there were so many, yet was not the net broken.

Why 153? Most modern theologians question whether the Saint had any cryptic meaning, but Rami is much given to numerology and the like. There are, it seems, 153 uses of the Tetragrammaton in the book of Genesis. St Augustine was the first to point out some of the mathematical curiosities of the number – 153 is the sum of the first 17 integers. There have been countless other speculations along these lines, but the only historical certainty about this puzzle is that it has inspired Christians across the ages. When John Colet founded St Paul's School, London in 1512, for example, he intended it to teach 153 sons of poor families. Though much larger today, the school still has 153 Foundation Scholars.

Trudie, who knows her Biblical numerology, also points out that there is a tradition of interpretation which makes 153 the numerical equivalent of the phrase "Sons of God".

Richard takes over from Rami and speaks of John as "the most paradoxical of Gospels." For example, John 21:7:

> Therefore that disciple whom Jesus loved saith unto Peter, It is the Lord. Now, when Simon Peter heard that it was the Lord, he girt his fisher's coat unto him, (for he was naked,) and did cast himself into the sea.

Who on earth pulls on a coat to go swimming? Richard has no ready answer, and nor do we.

Behind me are on the coach is a married couple in their sixties, Mo and Bryan. Their evident deep affection for each other does not keep them from indulging in non-stop mocking banter, most of it aimed by the quick-witted Mo at Bryan. As we prepare to disembark:

Bryan: "I think I'm going to leave my bag on the bus."
Mo: "You really live on the edge, don't you, darling?"

Our next stage is an ancient city, and it is a thing of wonder.

Capharnaum: The Town of Jesus

That's how the road signs spell it, anyway. King James spells it "Capernum", and reference books tend to favour

"Capernaum". It is, anyway, a rendering of the Hebrew name Kfar Nahum – "Nahum's Village". However spelled it is the fishing village to which Christ came immediately upon leaving his home in Nazareth, and beginning his mission. As Luke has it (4:31)

> But he passing through the midst of them went his way. And came down to Capernum, a city of Galilee, and taught them on the Sabbath days. And they were astonished at his doctrine: for his word was with power.

These words were delivered in the Synagogue – not the so-called White Synagogue, which was constructed some time in the 4th or 5th centuries AD, but in the earlier structure which stood on exactly the same site.

Capernum was also the site of a number of the Saviour's miracles. He healed a man who had been possessed by an evil spirit; and according to one version, he was begged by a centurion to heal one of his servants. But Christ's ministry in the town did not end well, and he pronounced a formal curse on its inhabitants (Matt. 11:23). Matthew himself is thought to have lived here, and the apostles Simon Peter, Andrew, James and John to have lived only a mile or so away. All of the four Gospels give some account of Christ's time here.

Nowadays, Capernum is a sizeable collection of

ruins and remains, laid out for the most part in large rectangles. Among the scattered building blocks are a fair number of well-preserved walls, columns and decorative carvings, as well as a well-preserved olive press. Capernum was already about 200 years old when Christ came here, and it was inhabited until the eleventh century, after which it was left largely ignored until successive waves of archæologists from the UK, the USA, Italy and German dug it out of sands and brought it back to public gaze. The palms and the eucalyptus trees that made the fringes of the site so comfortably shady were planted by monks of the Franciscan order in the early twentieth century.

After one of Rami's historical briefings, which in me at least are beginning to provoke serious scepticism (he points to a carved motif with six points, and uses this as evidence that Israel's national sigil, the Star of David, is not in fact of exclusively Jewish provenance), we break up into small groups, wander around, take photographs. One of the more modest details that catches my eye is some rough, ragged scratch marks on a paving stone. Rami explains that it served as a kind of board for Roman soldiers, who played a game with pebbles on it. Small, almost insignificant human traces such as these often do more to bring the ancient past close than grand monuments. Easy to imagine the hands, two millennia ago, that threw the pebbles, to while away the boredom of a hot day.

Next up is a stroll down to the nearby shore, and on to a short boat trip.

On the Sea of Galilee

As we shuffle along the footpath, we see a pleasure boat flying the Stars and Stripes, and hear the brassy tones of the US national anthem belting out of loud-speakers. One or two of us smile a little at this robust flourish of patriotism – catch the British being so brazen! – but then the joke is on us, as our own boat runs up the Union Jack and blares out "God Save The Queen". It is a tricky moment for the easily embarrassed, torn between finding the whole display a little vulgar yet not wanting to seem lacking in loyalty to the Crown, nor ungrateful for what is, after all, meant to be a welcoming touch. Father Richard sets an example by standing to ramrod attention, and we gratefully follow suit.

Our boat trip lasts about an hour, and it is the most purely agreeable experience we have had so far. The sun is bright, the breezes are fresh, the cheesy music played over loudspeakers is more amusing than irritating and the crew are not unduly pushy in selling us souvenirs. Once more, Rami points out the hills where the "pig-shepherds" tended their herds. The faces of strangers are, day by day, becoming more familiar. There is something about being alone on the waves that advances the subtle adjustments that are making us more than just an assortment of individuals. The dazzling motion of light across the gentle waves makes the heart lift. I can only begin to speculate about how much richer this experience must be for my new friends, almost all of whom believe that their Saviour once walked on these calm waters.

Back on shore, it is time for lunch. I fall into conversation with a quiet and apparently rather shy young pilgrim named Kate, and am delighted to find that she loves the films of two (nowadays not so well known) directors I also admire: Robert Bresson and Carl Theodore Dreyer. We don't mention the fact, but both Bresson and Dreyer are often talked of in spiritual terms by their admirers. It makes me wonder yet again about the ways in which a sympathetic atheist can make sense of the human capacity, common to pretty much every culture, of spirituality.

Holy Mountain

The last major excursion of the day is to Holy Mountain – the place where Jesus preached the Sermon on the Mount, and outlined the Beatitudes.

"How many Beatitudes are there?" asks Rami. Only a few of us know the right answer: eight. (Actually, some theologians reckon them at ten, which was what I had guessed.) Both Luke and Matthew describe the Sermon on the Mount, though it is Matthew's formulation – Book Five, chapters 3-10 – which has become definitive.

Approach the Beatitudes simply as a work of rhetoric, and you will be struck by their elegantly plain balance of paradoxes. At the heart of the Sermon is a reversal or upending of conventional wisdom. Christ identifies eight classes of people, in each case those generally considered by the world to be wretched, weak or of small consequence, and maintains that these worldly losers are, in the eternal scheme of things, those who win. They are:

1. The poor in spirit.
2. Mourners.
3. The meek.
4. Those who hunger after righteousness.
5. The merciful.
6. The pure in heart.
7. Peacemakers
8. Those persecuted in the cause of righteousness.

Breaking the precise pattern slightly, Jesus adds (chapter 11):

> Blessed are ye, when men shall revile you, falsely,
> for my sake.

Richard lightens the mood with one of his theological quips: "We've got a two-for-one deal on plenary indulgences, one week only…"

For anyone whose visual impression of the Sermon on the Mount is founded primarily on Monty Python's *Life of Brian* – all heat and dust and rocks – the summit of the Holy Mountain will come as a delicious surprise. The church is surrounded by beautifully maintained gardens, as colourful, well-watered and neatly groomed as anything you will find in a Georgian country house, though with much more vivid hues, and bathed in a stronger light. It is the first such garden we will meet on our travels, and the last on such a grand scale until we reach our final stop, the even more ravishing grounds of Emmaus, in a week's time.

The only discordant note here is the presence of a couple of young American evangelicals – the girl so pretty and so scantily dressed that quite a few of the more red-blooded chaps immediately forget some of the other words Jesus spoke here ("But I say unto you, That whoever looketh on a woman to lust after her hath committed adultery with her already in his heart..."). But she is, it seems, acting as bait: bait for the kind of hunt for converts that is sometimes called "phishing". The young man or boy accompanying her is unpleasantly aggressive in his militant compassion. He spots our Mo – already so well-liked by all of us that she is being referred to with affection as "Queen Mo" or "Your Mojesty" – and takes note of her walking stick, frail body and careful gait. He swoops:

Young American: "May I pray over you?"

Mo: "No, you may not!"

Only mildly discouraged, he takes her firmly by the arm as if about to wrestle her to the ground and gabbles some kind of a prayer while she tries, politely but strenuously, to shake the importunate youth away. Once the initial annoyance has passed, Mo finds the event funny, and so do the rest of us. My dear, British pilgrims simply don't do such things…

That night, after dinner, we talk of many things, some of them inspired by the day's encounters and sights.

Transfiguration is a hot topic, as tomorrow we will be visiting the Church of the Transfiguration on Mount Tabor. I am not entirely sure I know what "transfiguration" means to Christians, so I drift off to my room to study it. My texts for the night are Matt. 17, 1-9; Mark 9, 2-8; and Luke 9, 28-36. This is not too demanding a reading list, and there is plenty of time to head back down to the garden for a nightcap.

Bethlehem

Half past seven in the morning. We board the coach for the trip from Galilee to Bethlehem, via Jericho, which will take most of the day. The landscape grows more harsh and desiccated the further we go into the south.

This morning, the topics for conversation begin on an entirely secular note. Father Richard introduces the theme of Posh Radar – that super-power possessed by (especially) British women of upper-middle-class standing, or better, that allows them to detect the precise degree of vulgarity in anyone even an inch or so below them on the social ladder. Richard suggests that one of his elderly female relatives had this power to an intense degree. Asked how she managed to keep her spirits up in her the depressing surroundings of a nursing home, she replied "Schadenfreude and Snobbery, dear…." The same relative regards the Duchess of Cambridge's mother as "common".

We head on into all manner of unexpected digressions, from the strange political career of Jeffrey Archer to the precise difference in nuance between the term "Locks" and "Tresses" Consensus: the former is an acceptable term for a certain style of hair, the latter is unacceptably corny.

We stop off at a service station. It costs two shekels for a pee, and few of us have any small change. After a bit of resource-pooling, everyone who needs it manages to find relief.

Within the larger pilgrim band we have begun to form smaller groups of people who enjoy each other's humour and like to engage in spirited banter. My peer group for the rest of the trip will usually be made up of Mo and Bryan, Helen, Nicholas and Colin, and Trudie. Trudie has a trait in common with Helen, who is her room-mate for the pilgrimage, and to an even more pronounced degree. She is that very English figure, a highly intelligent and thoughtful person who likes to pretend that she is an uncouth idiot. In reality, Trudie teaches philosophy at a Catholic school – her faith, I would guess from a few remarks she lets slip, is very strong – and when push comes to shove she can discuss the Kantian Categorical Imperative with the best of them. Her favourite game is to act like one of her more stroppy teenage charges, deriding others – well, me, mostly – for their pomposity and fancy words.

At the morning service, we make the Sign of Peace. I first encountered this when I was invited to a Catholic Mass at the age of about 19, on a trip to Italy. Having been used to Anglican ways, it took me a little by surprise when strangers began pumping my hand. Richard explains to me a little of the long history of this gesture, which grew out of the fairly common practise of men greeting men with a kiss. Christ himself and his followers sanctified the habit by giving the "Holy Kiss" – it's mentioned several times in the Gospels. With such impeccable credentials, the Holy Kiss became an integral part of Christian worship. In the words of Saint Augustine:

> … when the Sacrifice is finished, we say the Lord's Prayer, which you have received and recited. After this, the "peace be with you" is said, and the Christians embrace each other with the Holy Kiss. This is a sign of peace; as the lips indicate, let peace be made in your conscience, that when your lips draw close to those of your brother, do not let your heart withdraw from his."

In the twenty-first century the Kiss is more usually a cordial handshake and maybe a hug. We circulate, each of us seeking out the other twenty-four pilgrims, saying "Peace be with you" and adding Christian names if we know them. After four days together, I am fairly confident of about fifteen names, and many of the pilgrims know mine, smiling broadly as they make eye contact and pump my hand. Sara, my coach buddy, is Old School, and gives me not merely the Sign but the Kiss of Peace. In my more cynical youth, I might have found all this a bit cloying and fake. Today, I find it not simply pleasant, but unexpectedly moving.

Back on the coach, some of us fall to talking about the Nativity. We moot the idea that we should stage an impromptu Nativity Play in our Bethlehem hotel. (Nothing comes of this.)

Church of the Transfiguration, Mount Tabor

The next leg of the journey takes us up a steeply inclined, alarmingly winding road. Before long we are so high up that we look down on birds in flight – and a single plane, which Helen, the aviation buff, identifies as a type of Cessna.

Our destination is a large, impressive church built in the early twentieth century, on the ruins of a Crusader castle that had been destroyed by Saladin, by an Italian architect – Antonio Barluzzi (1884-1960). Father Barluzzi, who has with justice been called "the architect of the Holy Land", is an extraordinary and rather attractive figure, who by the end of his life was showered with all manner of medals and awards, but conducted himself with modesty and restraint, living the straightforward life of the Franciscan monk he was. Barluzzi showed early signs of his architectural vocation by producing remarkably detailed drawings of churches when he was only five years old. He built and/or restored some 24 major buildings in the Holy Land – churches, schools, hospitals – and we will be seeing a lot more of his work soon.

Authorities continue to dispute the matter, but the consensus is that this is the site of what Aquinas called the greatest of all miracles: the Transfiguration of Christ. The Transfiguration is unique among the miracles recorded in the Synoptic Gospels because it happens to Christ rather than because of Him. Briefly, the disciples see Christ's body blazing with wondrous light; he confers with the two greatest Old Testament prophets, Moses and Elijah, implicitly taking precedence over both of them; and then the Voice of God – Jehovah, Yahweh, what you will – pronounces that Christ is His Son.

There was a Byzantine church here from the 4th to 6th centuries AD, but the modern church is mostly constructed with regard to the original forms of the Crusader buildings. There are three small grottoes, taken over from the Crusader structures, which alluded to the three huts which Peter wanted to build for Christ, Moses and Elijah. High up on the walls is a rather magnificent mosaic on a gold ground, representing the miracle; Barluzzi arranged for a window to be placed opposite it, so that it is brilliantly illuminated at midday on August 6 each year – the Day of Transfiguration. "Lush!", says Helen; and lush it is.

Outside the church there is a gathering of young IDF soldiers, taking a break from an exercise – or so we guess, from the powerful smell of unwashed bodies. The fit young lads lounge around in the sunlight, most of them bare-chested. Richard murmurs to me that he finds the sight rather tantalising; he has a bit of a penchant for slender young Mediterranean types. Colin joins us and begins to reminisce about his time in the Territorial Army, and how hard it had been to come out to his brothers in arms. Rami, to my surprise, tells us that he had volunteered for the IDF and served two years. It was a pragmatic, not an ideological decision – IFT veterans have superior opportunities in education, housing…

"Buddy Call!"

✠ ✠ ✠ ✠

Back on the coach. Erica moves down the aisle, proffering fruit: "Anyone for a date?" Father David, who trained as a nurse before deciding to take Holy Orders, tells an amusing story of once having encountered a Very Famous Singer when he was doing triage at the A & E unit of the Mount Sinai hospital in Los Angeles.

"She came in complaining of a sore throat – claimed not to be able to speak and had a flunky speak for her. She had her head wrapped in a scarf and never made eye-contact with me…"

Richard tells the mildly ghoulish story of how at one time he used to hitch rides to work in the cabin of a hospital vehicle which was used to deliver fresh corpses to a local undertakers'. The driver was a large, solemn Jamaican chap who seldom spoke a word, until one day, he said: ""Father Richard…" "Yes?". The driver motioned behind him with a nod of the head towards their deceased passenger: "Jeremy Beadle in back…" – Mr Beadle was a fairly well-known presenter of tacky, down-market television quizzes.

One of the great passions of Father Richard's later years has been Wagner. (Father David cannot stand Wagner. This domestic rift seems to be the fate of many Wagnerians, I have found.) He came to Wagner late, as he came to Christianity late, and now loves Wagner's operas so much that he has even given his man-shed in their Finedon garden a Wagnerian name: Wahnfried. As we head on towards our lunch, he tells us the not-many-people-know-that fact that the Dragon which was part of the stage furniture for the first staging of the Ring cycle in Bayreuth was manufactured in Clapham…

We arrive at the West Bank border. To our left: the Jordanian mountains. Ahead of us: Jericho.

Jericho

Some historians believe that Jericho might be the oldest continually inhabited city in the world; archæologists have uncovered evidence of buildings that are roughly eleven thousand years old. Geographers, more certain of their facts, tell us that it is the lowest-lying city in the world.

Jericho is, as you will recall if you know your Old Testament, the first of the cities taken by the Israeli army in their conquest of Canaan. As the Book of Joshua (6:1-17) records, the Israelites besieged the place for six days, parading the Ark of the Covenant around its walls; on the seventh day, seven priests sound their trumpets of ram's horn, and the soldiers, following Joshua's orders, shouted in unison, causing the walls to collapse.

> And they utterly destroyed all that was in the city, both man and woman, young and old, and ox, and sheep, and ass, with the edge of the sword... And they burnt the city with fire, and all that was within....

Or in, in the more familiar words, from the Spiritual:

> Joshua fit the Battle of Jericho
> And the walls came tumblin' down...

Today, there is little sign of antiquity, and our main interest in stopping here is to have an al fresco lunch, at the Al Rawdah Garden Restaurant. It has the air of a place that has seen better days – the swimming pool is dry – but the skewers of juicy meat kebabs are the tastiest food we've had so far. A solo parrot stares down on us as we munch. John Patrick – "JP" – complains that an anonymous poster on Twitter has been saying irreverent things about his conduct on pilgrimage. Trudie gleefully confesses that it is she who has been tweeting the rude updates. For some imponderable reason, the talk turns to wombats.

Back on the bus. We will not be going to Jacob's Well because it is too dangerous today. In Hebron, a 15-year-old boy has been shot dead by the IDF, and his two brothers imprisoned. It is grim news, and prompts Rami into some of his darker musings. The wilderness we are driving through, he says, was once a place which the Bedouins took as their own. But they were driven away.

Next stop: the town where Christ was born.

Bethlehem

> O little town of Bethlehem,
> How still we see the lie,
> Above thy deep and dreamless sleep,
> The silent stars go by.

Yet in thy dark streets shineth,
The everlasting light,
The hopes and fears of all the years,
Are met in thee tonight.

Well, it's hardly a little town these days, and its crammed streets are far from silent, and the first glimpse of it ahead speaks more loudly of conflict than of peace. The whole city is enclosed within a high wall of gray concrete. There are security cameras, barbed wire, troops with assault rifles. Easy to see why some citizens call it an open-air prison. At the first security checkpoint, we see an Arab shepherd in twenty-first century Western clothes, herding his sheep through the guards. In a film, it would seem like a corny piece of symbolism. "While shepherds watched their flocks…"

Bethlehem has been under Palestinian control since 1995, when the Israelis withdrew. One might have thought that this would be a development to gladden Rami's heart, since he seldom has anything but harsh things to say about Israel. But this is to forget the essential fact that he is a Palestinian Christian, not a Muslim. He launches into a tirade about the worthlessness of the local government, the Palestinian National Authority, which he angrily calls "Palestinian Nothing Authority" – "I feel like I want to vomit." He has nothing but contempt for the PNA, who, he insists, have failed to build anything since 1995. They prefer not to re-house the refugees some of whom have been here since 1967, or even since 1948, and who live in squalid, insanitary camps.

Our driver shows exemplary skill in weaving our large coach through steep, narrow streets dense with parked and moving cars. Eventually he pulls up next to a sign saying "Sklep". It's a Polish grocery store, right in the heart of Jerusalem! For a few seconds I feel a mild stab of nostalgia for West London, where my Polish friends buy their favourite imported produce in stores just like this.

Rami leads us on a short walk up the hill to a souvenir shop. As on many guided tours, everywhere in the world, there is clearly some kind of you-scratch-my-back arrangement here, but we are for the most part willing dupes; some of us positively eager dupes. This is the first occasion on which we begin to note Nicholas's almost pathologically intense appetite for picking up souvenirs. He takes the ribbing in good part, and explains that he has promised to bring little gifts home for some absurd number of his fellow church-goers in Manchester.

The men who run the souvenir store have a good line in sales patter, though to British ears their conspicuous gallantry towards women sounds more than a trifle corny: "… And for our beautiful ladies here we have some fine jewels…" A few eyes are rolled, but we hold our peace.

The shopkeepers also have one exceptionally good yarn, all about the discovery of the Dead Sea Scrolls, not far from here. In a few words, what happened is that the young boys who accidentally found them had not the faintest idea of the true nature of the scrolls, but noticed that some of them had been engraved on leather. Seeing the chance for a quick profit, they brought the leather to a local shoemaker and minor dealer in antiquities – the grandfather of one of the men who now run the shop. The shoemaker was educated enough to suspect that these strips might have some significance; he contacted local scholars; and so they were saved. Photographs of the enlightened shoemaker hang above the display cabinets.

A few others join Nicholas in making their purchases, and then it is only a few minutes to our Bethlehem hotel, which stands just on the corner of Manger Square, a very short walk from the Church of the Holy Nativity.

There is an amusing episode at reception. The management has booked Richard into the best single room in the hotel. Richard thanks them for the honour, but says that he is more than happy to share with Father David. The receptionist repeats that Richard has been given a single room. Richard repeats that he is happy to share with David. The receptionist, just a little more firmly, reminds Richard that he has been given a SINGLE room. Richard gives in…

The place is clean, dimly lit and a little on the Spartan side: the rooms have no decorations or any of the other amenities that modern travellers expect – certainly no television. The touch of asceticism seems the right thing for pilgrims; a reminder that this is not just a holiday, however much it might feel that way at times. I gaze out of the window for a while, taking in the sight of the town as dusk deepens. At six o'clock comes an aural reminder that this is a city of ancient faiths as well as modern buildings: the first cry of the muezzin, calling the believers to prayer.

There is no set agenda for our pilgrim band this evening, but after the forgettable dinner most of us wander over to admire the exterior of the Church of the Holy Nativity, which was built, according to tradition, on top of site where Jesus was born. We venture inside. The aisles are quite dark, but the vault high above us is illuminated here and there by the moderate light of candles and the sharp beams from spotlights; in front of us, where a service is in progress, the area around the altar is warm and bright. The contrasts of murk and brilliance remind me of Ezra Pound's evocation of St Mark's, Venice. "In the gloom, the gold gathers the light against it…" But the real investigation of this holy place will be tomorrow.

Time for dinner, and then, for those who enjoy such things, drink and banter in the bar.

DAY FIVE: FRIDAY 21 MARCH 2014

Our first stop today will be the place where, according to tradition, the shepherds were met by the Angel of the Lord.

We board our coach at about eight, and are soon given another demonstration of our driver's remarkable skill in negotiating steep, narrow and crowded streets in a large vehicle. Once again, most of the buildings we pass are fairly recently built, and many of them bear the same motif on their walls or by their doors: a holy warrior on horseback, striking down a serpent. I initially assume that this represents St Michael's struggle with the Devil, but the reality is much more obvious, or should be for an Englishman. It is St George and the Dragon, George being the patron saint not only of England but of Bethlehem.

En route, Rami tells an elaborate political joke about a Palestinian donkey. I am not the only one who fails to understand it. We laugh politely anyway.

The Shepherd's Fields

Again, this is the work of Antonio Barluzzi, who constructed it in 1953-54. The design, simple but satisfying, is inspired by a Bedouin tent. It's polygonal, with five straight and five projecting sides. On the walls are fifteen frescoes by Barluzzi's friend Umberto Noni, representing scenes from the Annunciation to the arrival of the Holy Family in Egypt. The sand for these frescoes was brought here from the Sea of Galilee; a difficult trip at the time, as the military situation restricted transport to the Top Brass. Barluzzi got round the problem by hiring a chauffeur-driven limousine, which went to and from Galilee to the construction site with sandbags on the back seat. He used a good deal of glass in the ceiling, so that it is flooded with light by day, and you can gaze up at the stars by night.

For anyone who attended Christian schools in the United Kingdom, it is impossible not to be reminded of early childhood, and the oddly potent sound of girls and boys joined in Christmas carols:

> While Shepherds watched their flocks by night,
>   All seated on the ground,
> The angel of the Lord came down,
>   And glory shone around.

This sung version of events stays fairly loyal to Luke 2: 8-20.

> And there were in the same country shepherds abiding in the field, keeping watch over their flock by night. And lo, the angel of the Lord came upon them, and the glory of the Lord shone round about them: and they were sore afraid...

We listen to this very reading, and then we sing, and then we pray, and finally we sing another carol that takes us all back to childhood:

> Silent Night, Holy Night
> All is calm, all is bright,
> Round yon virgin Mother and Child,
> Holy infant so tender and mild,
> Sleep in heavenly peace,
> Sleep in heavenly peace…

Rami tells us that shepherds of New Testament times were by no means poor – their flocks were valuable commodities, as desirable as land – and they were not required to pay taxes. Father David joins in with a nugget from his theological studies: the familiar motif of a shepherd carrying a lamb on his shoulders is not quite as sweet as it appears: shepherds would deliberately injure the legs of their flocks, then tend them carefully until they were able to walk again, but only slowly and for short distances.

We head back into the heart of Bethlehem, and to the

Church of the Holy Nativity (1)

This is one of the most sacred sites in the world, since tradition tells us that it was constructed on top of the cave where Mary gave birth to Jesus. The church was originally built three centuries or so after her labour, in the years 327-339 AD, and on the orders of the Emperor Constantine and his mother Helena. It was one of the very first large-scale Christian churches, and its architectural style was inspired by the previously secular Roman form of the basilica – of which the key elements, easily seen here, are a large, high-ceilinged middle space, the nave, flanked on each side by a colonnaded aisle.

Constantine's basilica stood until the sixth century, when it was destroyed in the course of a violent uprising by the Samaritans. The Emperor Justinian ordered it rebuilt in 565 AD, and – barring various additions – it remained much the same for well over a thousand years. It was ruined in the Jerusalem earthquake of 1834, and then fell victim to years of architectural looting.

Rami tells us this orthodox history, adding his own spins and observations along the way. I scribble down as much as I can of his rapid-fire commentary. Some of them are unintelligible, but a few are clear enough:

> The "Jewish Scripture" – the Old Testament – spoke of a "star rising in Bethlehem." The star mentioned in the Gospels is thus one of the many fulfilments of prophecy.
>
> Jesus Christ was born fourteen generations after David.

He only became known as Jesus "of Nazareth" after Palm Sunday.

The word "Nazarene" can also signify "the stem". Hence: Jesus the stem. The book of Isaiah speaks of a "shoot of Jesse".

At the Crucifixion, there was an earthquake which brought down the wall of the Temple in Jerusalem. Henceforth – no more barrier between God and man.

The sacrifice of Christ replaces the sacrifice of animals.

During the Persian occupation of the Holy Land, the invading army noted images of the Magi in this church, and, recognising their Persian clothes, spared the place from destruction and looting.

"The Jews are still expecting the Messiah."

Unfortunately, the queues are too long for us to pay our visit to the grotto of Christ's birth, beneath the altar, so we decide to come back this evening, and, for the time being, go instead down a set of steps to see the:

Cave of Saint Jerome

These caves, beneath the Church, are where Jerome (*c.* 347-420 AD) is said to have spent something like 34 years, from 388 onwards, translating both the Old and the New Testaments into Latin. (Other sources say that he actually lived and died not precisely here but a couple of miles away, in a monastery cell just on the outskirts of Bethlehem.) His literary output was astonishingly vast by the standards of any age, and included Biblical commentaries, letters, historical essays and the like. Jerome's Latin translation of the Bible became known as the Vulgate, and has been immensely influential in the development and the transmission of the Christian faith.

Jerome is an interesting if not altogether attractive figure. "A frightful fellow, but a good Latinist," says Richard. He seems to have been born in a place known to his age as Stridon, somewhere in the region we now call Dalmatia. When still little more than a boy, he travelled to Rome, where he learned Latin at the feet of the then-famous grammarian Ælius Donatus. The teenage Jerome lived a fairly wild and dissolute life, but he converted to Christianity in his early twenties and bitterly regretted his rowdy youth.

For the next few years he travelled extensively around the middle east, becoming ordained en route, then returned to Rome where he began to learn Hebrew from a converted Jew. He began his great task of bringing the Bible to readers of Latin by translating the New Testament from the Greek; then he took on the much more challenging feat of translating the Old Testament from Hebrew. Up to this time, those who could not read Hebrew knew the Old Testament almost wholly from the Koine Greek translation known as the Septuagint.

This melodious name has the no-nonsense meaning of "Seven Times Ten", since the story has it that it was commissioned by Ptolemy II (reigned 283 BC to 246 BC), who sought out 70 (in some versions, 72) Jewish wise men. Ptolemy asked them to translate the "Torah of your leader Moshe [Moses]" so that a version could be deposited in the Library of Alexandria. Whether or not this is true, the dating of third century BC seems about right; and the Septuagint, made up of the five first Old Testament books – Genesis, Exodus, Leviticus, Numbers and Deuteronomy – was the most widely read version of the Pentateuch amongst non-Hebrew speakers for about 600 years. It is cited a number of times in the New Testament.

These small caves beneath the Church have been preserved more or less by accident, since, under Hadrian's persecution of Christians (c. 135 AD), a series of Roman temples were built on top of former places of worship, thus sealing them up intact for centuries. Hadrian's temple was devoted to the cult of Adonis; an interesting note for students of comparative religion.

Father Richard, who has spent years studying such arcane matters, explains to us that there are often differences between Vulgate and original, some obvious, others only apparent to those who have a profound knowledge of the original languages. For example, Christ's famous rebuke to Mary Magdalene in John 20:17 is, in the Vulgate: "Noli me tangere" – "Do not touch me". This appears to be the emotion expressed, for example, in Titian's version of the encounter. But, Richard says, the Koine Greek original – *me mou haptu* – means something more like "Do not cling to me."

As anyone with a passing knowledge of Italian art will know, Jerome has been painted many, many times, and as a result is by far the most familiar of the four great Doctors of the Church – the others being Augustine of Hippo, Ambrose and Gregory I. I ask Richard about the familiar iconography of Jerome and the Lion – a detail which always, to me at least, makes the saint seem sympathetic and appealing. ("Look – He had a great big pussy cat!") Richard explains that this convention was quite a late addition to the iconographic tradition, and probably arose from a confusion between Jerome and another saint of fairly similar name, one Gerasimus (d. 475), who is said to have tamed a lion in the wilderness after pulling a thorn from its paw; in other words, exactly what Androcles does with his lion in the Roman folk tale, which appears to date from the second century AD.

The topic of nastiness in some of the Church Fathers prompts me to ask Richard about Tertullian (*c.* 155 - *c.* 240 AD), to my mind a surprisingly sinister figure, a profound misogynist even by the standards of his times, and notorious for having written that one of the pleasures enjoyed by the souls of the blessed in Heaven is the sadistic one of gazing down on those burning in Hell and gloating.

Richard nods, agreeing that this is a hard doctrine to stomach.

"They weren't cute, the Church Fathers."

It is time for a coffee break, but all this heavy-duty theology is addictive, so we keep up the Q & A discussions. Perhaps to cleanse our spiritual palates a bit after having dwelled on the decidedly un-cute Jerome and Tertullian, Richard cites a delightful maxim from one of his favourite saints, Irenæus.

"The Glory of God is a human being fully alive."

Amen.

The Holy Family Hospital

Some of the money we have spent to come on this pilgrimage has been by way of donations to some local Christian charities. This afternoon's visits will show us some of the work that these charities are doing within Bethlehem. The first stop is the Holy Family Hospital – Motto: "The Poorest deserve the Best" – which is dedicated to "providing quality care for women and infants, without regard to religion or national origins." This admirably open-minded policy has had the predictable result – most of their patients are very poor Palestinian Arabs. They like to point out the powerful symbolism of the fact that they are just "800 meters from the birthplace of Christ…" The hospital is run by a Catholic charity, the Sovereign Order of Malta.

As we wait for our guide to take us on a tour, we try to communicate a little with the casually dressed young Palestinian men in the corridor, waiting for their wives to give birth to the baby sisters and brothers of the toddlers who are running around our feet. The chaps are cheerful and friendly, and seem to enjoy seeing us playing silly games with their kids, and giving them sweets.

After quite a long wait, we are joined by our host, who is the chief paediatrician here, and is a highly accomplished man wearing a smart suit. There are a couple of remarkable things about him: one is that he was himself born in this hospital. He is also what we nowadays tend to call a Small Person; earlier generations would have called him a midget.

He gives us a talk. Some of it is proud statistics: the hospital has cared for more than 55,000 mothers, without a single incident of maternal death; the standards of care are well up to Western standards. They carry out 23,000 post-natal examinations a year through an outreach programme which includes health education. And then there are the grim statistics: Bethlehem has no social security system, no medical insurance schemes, and, with a 27 per cent unemployment rate, very few citizens can afford to pay for treatment. The hospital is almost wholly dependent on donations. If you'd like to contribute, their bank account is Holy Family Hospital, Account No. 389000, Bank of Palestine PLC.

Father Richard presides over a Eucharist in the hospital's chapel.

Palestinian Christian Cultural Centre

The other local charity we have helped to fund is a Lutheran organisation called Diyar – the plural form of the Arabic word dar, which can mean either "home" or "homeland". It announces its "vision" as helping local people "to have life more abundantly". The inspiration is John 10:10:

> The thief cometh not, but for to steal, and to kill, and to destroy: I am come that they might have life, and that they might have it more abundantly.

Founded in 1995, Diyar is one of the few success stories of this unhappy city. Among its activities are: teaching children to paint, draw and play musical instruments (we see several earnest youngsters toting their instruments to class); encouraging women and girls to take part in sports; publishing books on Palestinian subjects; and caring for the elderly – most of those over the age of 65 here have no form of health insurance or social security. About half the population of Bethlehem is young – under twenty – and unemployed, and bitter.

We head for the chapel, where we are addressed by a gently spoken young woman who must be some-where in her late twenties. It is not primarily a political speech, though she does begin by ruefully comparing the present condition of Israel to a Swiss cheese – "Is-rael has the cheese; we have the holes." and ends by glumly observing that "even as we speak, the land is shrinking." It is hard to scrape together an education, hard to find a job, hard to avoid feeling that, as an Arab Christian, you are hated by both sides.

But, she insists: "Here, with Diyar, it is more a story of hope." The wall is always there, but, she says, they are trying to tell their youngsters not to despair but to look upwards:

"Not to see the wall, but to see the sky."

We buy some of the products in their souvenir shop – including jewellery made from glass broken in local conflicts – and leave wishing them well.

✠ ✠ ✠ ✠

Thus far I have deliberately not sought out Richard's company, realising that his first obligation is to his

64

Father Coles in Nazareth, first stop

*Open air mass at the edge of the
Sea of Galilee*

Stone carving at Capharnaum

*Opposite: Why 153? Father Coles discusses
numerology on the beach at Galilee*

Church of the Angels by Antonio Barluzzi, Shepherds' Fields

Hebron

Gethsemane, garden at the foot of the Mount of Olives, Jerusalem

Mount of Olives, Jerusalem

On the road in Jerusalem

Opposite: Souk, Jerusalem

parishioners; anyway, it has been fun to sit with new people at each meal, and enjoy learning a little about them. But Richard now has a spare hour or so to indulge me, and we wander off in search of refreshment. We choose a small, open-fronted juice bar, cheekily painted up to resemble a well-known American chain of coffee shops, and order freshly squeezed pomegranate juice – which is chilled, tangy and not too sweet.

A middle-aged man sidles up to us. We assume he is going to ask us for money; but no. "English?", he asks us. We admit that we are indeed English. He then repeats a well-known slander about Welsh farmers and their excessive fondness for their flocks; shrieks with laughter and rushes away. Richard and I ponder a while on the strange pathways of cultural and racial stereotypes; then talk a little about the ways in which the British think about priests and churches and faith. I've noticed that Richard hardly ever utters more than the mildest profanity when he is with his flock; but when we are on our own he enjoys potty-mouthed humour as much as I do.

I tell him an anecdote about an Army church parade, which I heard from the brother of a regimental padre. It has the C-bomb as its punch-line, and it makes Richard laugh until he weeps. It reminds him of an incident when, in full clerical regalia, he led a procession through the streets of a district in South London, and an angry drunk threw a box of fried chicken at him, while yelling the very same word. Before settling in Finedon, Richard had been appointed to some fairly tough parishes, and was taken aback to discover how much anger the sight of a dog-collar can provoke among the marginal and the dispossessed. (Mind you, he also spent a few years at a church in London's poshest district, Knightsbridge.)

The talk turns to charity, and the giving of alms to the poor. I am slightly surprised to hear that Richard has developed a hard line on handouts. Ever since the first time I read Samuel Johnson's reply to prim souls who felt that one should never give pennies to beggars since they will only spend it on drink ("He who makes a beast of himself gets rid of the pain of being a man"), I have never though twice about digging into my pocket for a homeless person. Richard's time in mean districts, though, has taught him that all too often one's pounds and pence are used to buy something worse than booze: heroin. These days, Richard offers to buy those who approach him a meal in a fast food joint, and to learn something of their lives and plights as they eat. They are often as glad for the chance to tell someone their story as they are for the grub.

Something to ponder, again.

Church of the Holy Nativity (2)

At exactly 5.20 pm, we head back to the Church of the

Holy Nativity, where a Greek Orthodox service is in progress. The queue for the Grotto of the Nativity is long – there must be a good four hundred people or so here, maybe more – and it moves slowly. It takes us slightly more than half an hour of shuffling forwards, pausing, shuffling again to reach the entrance. Throughout the wait, we are all being policed by a single Orthodox monk sporting John Lennon spectacles, a patriarchal beard, a scowl and a major bad temper. He growls and curses at anyone who so much as speaks above the most delicate whisper; which would be fair enough, were the service being conducted to reverent silence from the faithful. In reality, the young children of the Orthodox congregation, thronged in a space to the right of the altar, are doing what young children almost everywhere on our planet do best: making an ear-tormenting racket that would not be drowned out by a jet taking off. Compared to them, we are like a convention of Trappists.

After about twenty minutes, one of our pilgrims makes the mistake of chuckling lightly at a joke, at exactly the same moment that someone a few rows behind us starts shouting. Mistaking the culprit, Lennon zooms in on her, grabs her by the arm and shouts and shouts at her furiously as he tries to drag her out of the church. This calls for an act of gallantry, and Father David steps forward. He puts himself between Lennon and the pilgrim, who continues to scream about people making irreverent noise. David, calmly but firmly: "It seems to me that YOU are making most of the noise…" It's doubtful that Lennon entirely grasps the irony of his behaviour, but, still, he wanders away muttering grimly.

After such a long wait, anti-climax. Closing time is near, and the Church wardens make us rush down into the Grotto and then out again at such a rapid pace that the more nimble of us are almost running. Candles blaze on all sides. The shrine itself proves to be little more than a hole in a slab of granite, with ornate silver carvings around it in the form of a fourteen-pointed star, and a collection of silver lamps. It is traditional to lie down and reach into the hole to touch a rock that marks the exact site of the Virgin's labour, but I decide not to indulge, especially as Richard has murmured to me that scholars mostly agree that it is highly unlikely that this part of the church does indeed Mark The Spot.

Back to the hotel for another bland dinner. Mo has been so upset by the nasty behaviour of the monk that I ply her with drinks and daft stories until she cheers up. One by one, the more fun-loving pilgrims gather in the bar, where a bottle of perfectly quaffable Star of David dry white wine costs 350 shekels. Nicholas has missed our set meal – too busy hunting for souvenir shops, probably – but the ever-thoughtful Mo has ordered a pizza for him.

David and Richard have changed into mufti for

the evening. David, cheerfully smoking, keeps urging Richard on to play a few tunes on the bar's piano, but Richard's resists the blandishments until a couple of whiskies have sufficiently loosened his inhibitions and his fingers. Finally, he treats us to some fancy improvisations, mostly in a jazzy style. Impressive! This man could probably be a professional musician, if he wanted.

Tomorrow, some of us will feel just a little under the weather.

Jerusalem (1)

DAY SIX: SATURDAY 22 MARCH
BETHANY: THE TOMB OF LAZARUS
JORDAN RIVER
MOUNT TEMPTATION
KALIA BEACH
INTO JERUSALEM

We leave Bethlehem early, to set out on the road to Jerusalem.

The first stop on today's trip will be the Tomb of Lazarus and the house of Mary and Martha, in Bethany.

The on-board choice of music is decidedly cheesy. Someone has the poor taste to play a novelty hit from the early seventies – "Knock Three Times" (I cannot recall the name of the artistes, and decline to investigate). This leads to talk of the Hit Parade, and of Richard's triumphs as a teen idol in the mid 1980s.

Rami, who has until now had no idea about Richard's past as a pop star, thinks at first that we are all conspiring to rib him; then breaks into a massive grin as he realises that we aren't. Someone whips out a tablet and summons up the Communard's greatest hit,

70

their spirited cover of the Motown classic *Don't Leave Me This Way*. We all join in with the chorus. What larks! It's a great song.

Bethany

This modest town is one of the most important places in the New Testament. Five events are recorded:

1. Christ raised Lazarus from the dead.
2. Christ set off from Bethany to Jerusalem on Palm Sunday.
3. Christ lodged here during the week after Palm Sunday.
4. Mary anointed Christ at a dinner.
5. Christ ascended into Heaven.

Father Richard refers us the Velazquez painting of *Mary and Martha* in the National Gallery, London.

The episode is recorded in John 11:1-54, which begins:

> Now a certain man was sick, named Lazarus, of Bethany, the town of Mary and her sister Martha (It was that Mary which anointed the Lord with ointment, and wiped his feet with her hair, whose brother Lazarus was sick.)…

The traditional site of the cave where Christ revived Lazarus is now covered by the al-Uzar mosque, constructed by the Ottomans in the 16th century.

Rami tells us that that in Islam, Lazarus is "one of 27 important prophets". But one can gain access to the tomb by means of a Catholic church – the work, again, of the ubiquitous Antonio Barluzzi, who completed this building in 1952-3, just before starting work on the Shepherds' Fields.

> Then when Jesus came, he found that he had lain in the grave for four days already…

Rami: why does the text specify that Lazarus had been dead for four days? Because it was believed that the soul leaves the body after three days.

> Jesus said unto her, I am the resurrection, and the life: he that believeth in me, though he were dead, yet shall he live…

Rami reminds us that Christ performed three miracles in or near Jerusalem:

1. Raising Lazarus from the dead.
2. Healing the crippled man at the Pool of Bethesda.
3. Healing the blind.

As so often, Rami's discourse is a piquant mixture of contemporary political commentary, biblical history and idiosyncratic scholarship, plus the occasional wince-making dig at Jewish people. I wonder briefly if I should ask him to knock off the anti-Semitic "jokes", but decide that there is a time to keep silent. Of

Bethany today, Rami observes that there are no police here. "They are afraid". He also says that there is, in effect, no local government, either. But when he speaks of the "Occupation", he means the Romans, not the Israelis.

From the Crusader section of the Church, there is a panoramic view of the Judæan desert. Down inside the cave, it is pleasantly cool – the effect of an ingenious early technology of air circulation to keep the temperature comfortable.

> And he that was dead came forth, bound hand and foot with graveclothes: and his face was bound about with a napkin.

The most interesting point Rami makes is that it was the act of bringing Lazarus back from the dead that precipitated the death of Jesus.

> But some of them went their ways to the Pharisees, and told them what things Jesus had done...

The Pharisees spotted a major political danger here. If Jesus were allowed to carry on working miracles, it will not be long before the masses accept him as a messiah:

> ... and the Romans shall come and take away both our place and nation.

Caiaphas, the high priest, tells his followers that this is

a disaster they must avert. They can accomplish it with very little effort. Jesus must die.

> Then from that day forth they took counsel together for to put him to death...

The shortest verse in the New Testament is John 11:35:

> Jesus wept.

Outside, we rejoin Rami, who has filled the palm of his hand with mustard seeds. He shows them then nods towards the tree from which he gathered them. "Seeds... Tree..." He is reminding us of the shortest parable in the New Testament, from Mark 4:30-32, in which Christ offers a simile to explain the nature of the Kingdom:

> It is like a grain of mustard seed, which, when it is sown in the earth, is less that all the seeds that be in the earth: but when it is sown, it growth up, and becometh greater than all herbs, and shooteth out great branches; so that the fowls of the air may lodge under the shadow of it.

Like all the parables, this may be glossed in several ways. For Trudie, the central meanings are "that great things can be achieved by the smallest and weakest... and those things benefit not only the small and weak but others, too..." I am beginning to realise that Trudie's knowledge of the Bible is really quite profound.

Jordan River

Tradition has it that the point on the river bank which we are about to visit is very close to the exact place where John baptized Jesus, and possibly even the place itself. Apart from noting its significance in the narrative of Christ's life, we are also here to allow the faithful among us to renew their baptismal vows. Matthew 4:13-15:

> Then cometh Jesus from Galilee to Jordan unto John, to be baptized of him. But John forbad him, saying, I have need to be baptized of thee, and comest thou to me? And Jesus answering said unto him, Suffer it to be so now: for thus it becometh us to fulfil all righteousness. Then he suffered him.

The land is flat, and dusty, and so dry that it is hard to believe that we are only yards away from the legendary river.

> River of Jordan is deep and wide
> Hallelujah!
> Milk and Honey on the other side...

Hence one version of the great negro spiritual "Michael, Row The Boat Ashore", the one that I learned as a child. For decades it was transmitted orally, which is one reason why it exists in many versions, some of which do not even rhyme. The song was covered by countless artists in the early 1960s, as the American Civil Rights movement looked back for inspiration to the rich musical culture of African-Americans in the years following the civil war. As became obvious, the spirituals fused traditional Christian lore with a coded language about the harsh journey from slavery to freedom.

It is now close to 11 am, and it is starting to become very hot for those of us used to cool, damp England. Some of the other visitors sport white robes. Franciscans? Curious detail: for the first time on the trip, there are lots of information signs here in Russian – it would seem that the place is a magnet for visitors from the former USSR. And also for enthusiastic Israeli patriots and Zionists: the trinket store sells piles and piles of T-shirts with cocksure and not entirely tasteful jokes about the invincibility of the Israeli Defence Force.

It's a short walk to the river bank, which is thick with green foliage – very different from the parched surroundings. I take off my shoes and socks and paddle a little. The water, roughly the colour of strong coffee with a dash of milk, is unexpectedly cold. So the other words of the Spiritual were right:

> River of Jordan, chilly and cold
> Hallelujah!
> Chills the body, but not the soul
> Hallelujah!

On both sides of the bank, there are armed soldiers with weapons held at low port. Nicholas shakes his head sadly. "They are so out of place amidst all this holy activity…"

Trudie also comments wryly on the different national characters of pilgrims. There are lots of cheery young Americans here today, laughing, playing guitars, giving spontaneous shouts of "Alleluia!" and, when the time comes for being baptised, throw themselves head-first into the chill and muddy waters so that they experience total immersion.

By contrast, those in our group who mean to renew their baptismal vows here have no more than a modest paddle, and then wait in line patiently to read out a brief set of vows from a sheet of paper (provided) to Father Richard and Father David, both of them visibly uncomfortable in their black clericals as the heat rises and rises. One by one, the pilgrims come forward and answer a catechism:

Do you reject the Devil and all rebellion against God?
    I reject them.
Do you renounce the deceit and the corruption of evil?
    I renounce them…

Where the Americans use the waters of the Jordan to bring out their spiritual rebirth, we British are using drops of oil of chrism that we have brought with us. "Mad Dogs and Englishmen!" Trudie chuckles. But if the waters of the Jordan are too muddy for ceremonial use today, a few of the pilgrims fill small jars and bottles to collect the tan fluid for use at home. Months later, Mo tells me that she used her bottle at the christening of a new grandson.

Baptisms done, we pose for a group photograph – the only one of the whole trip. There is just one absentee. Somehow JP manages to slip away on some private mission. Those who know say that such elusiveness is typical of him. If we look more than conventionally happy in the resulting snap, it might be because we have now fully bonded into a kind of extended family group, where, as Mo put in a note written nicely a few months later, "the diversity and strength of those with faith were never challenged by those who had little or no faith. The group acted as one through all the rituals and services we went through, which I think was no mean achievement. Even after late night drinks as the bar there were no horrid 'shouty' arguments!"

Long-lasting friendships have been forged.

✠ ✠ ✠ ✠

We drive through Jericho again. According to Rami, the name Jericho literally means "The Good Smell", which in turn means the smell of balsam. Rami reminds us that Jesus called Jericho "cursed". He also reminds us of two of the minor New Testament characters who lived here. The first is Zacchaeus, who appears in Luke 19.

> And he sought to see Jesus who he was; and could not for the press, because he was little of stature.
> And he ran before, and climbed up into a sycamore tree to see him: for he was to pass that way.

Then there was also the woman who touched Christ, so that "the virtue went out of Him," Mark 5, 30:

> And Jesus, immediately knowing in himself that virtue had gone out of him, turned about in the press, and said, Who touched my clothes?

The land through which we are now driven runs through desert land. This is how one tends to imagine the wilderness of Old and New Testaments.

Richard, who has been keeping an eye on the news to see how political and military developments might affect our itinerary tells that there is a fair chance that we will not be able to go to Jacob's Well at all; skirmishes between the IDF and Palestinian forces have continued since the shooting in Hebron of the 15-year-old Palestinian boy two days ago.

Rami tells us more about recent political history.

Bedouins have been kicked off the land we are crossing. Bedouins, he reminds us, are not Arabs.

Mount Temptation

After a brief coach ride, we pull up to a parking lot. Ahead of us are steeply sloped high mountains – the site, according to Scripture, of the first two temptations of Christ by Satan. (The third temptation took place on the Temple Mount in Jerusalem.)

In the account of St. Luke, starting at Chapter 4: 1-3:

> And Jesus being full of the Holy Ghost returned from Jordan, and was led by the Spirit into the wilderness, being forty days tempted of the devil. And in those days he did eat nothing: and when they were ended, he afterward hungered. And the devil said unto him, If thou be the Son of God, command this stone that it may be made bread...

The sacred places on Mount Temptation are now administered by the Greek Orthodox Church, Rami tells us. It is usually possible to travel up to them; but today there is no time. Instead, we press on to the place where the Dead Sea Scrolls were discovered: Qumran.

Kalia Beach and the Dead Sea

The restaurant we were supposed to visit is full to over-flowing, so we head on to another one that is almost as packed with tourists – a self-service canteen-style place where you queue with trays for a limited choice of un-appetising food. We are close, here, to the place where the Dead Sea Scrolls were discovered; since the bread proves to be inedibly stale, there are cracks about eating "Dead Sea Rolls".

Fortified if not enchanted, we head on to the shore of the Sea itself: Kalia Beach. The weather is now hotter still, probably high eighties or thereabouts. Most of the pilgrims change into their modestly cut bathing cos-tumes and head for the famously saline waters, where they enjoy the sensation of being unable to sink. Richard, Helen and I decide to pull up beach chairs and enjoy a few cold ales. And then a few more. No sense in mortifying the flesh more than is strictly nec-essary.

The conversation is merry.

Richard: "Does anything live in the Dead Sea?"
Helen: "I think the clue might be in the name…"

After an hour or so, our friends come back to us, sopping wet and smeared with black mud – allegedly very good for the skin. The local gift shop sells Dead Sea skin products at what seem to me eye-watering prices, but some of the women pilgrims indulge, insisting that it is well worth the outlay.

We hold an outdoor service. The reading is from John, 4:

> I sent you to reap that whereon ye bestowed no labour: other men laboured, and ye are entered into their labours…

This reminds me of another John – the English radical writer John Berger, whose series of books about the lives of the poorest workers bears the collective title *Into Their Labours*. Christ, it strikes me for the thousandth time, was a God for the wretched of the earth. Weird that so many rich people make a show of following His teachings. Cognitive dissonance, or do they simply cherry-pick the scriptures for the most hateful interpretations? Both, probably.

Back on board the coach. Our next stop is the place that Europeans of the middle ages used to represent at the centre of their global maps, and which they believed to be by far the most important city in the world. Believers in the three Abrahamic religions feel the same way.

Jerusalem

Lulled by the afternoon beers, I take a snooze and the coach is already well inside the suburbs of Jerusalem when I am woken by anxious voices. To our left an ominous pillar of thick black smoke billows upwards. A missile strike? A little later, after we arrive at the hotel, David tells us that he has heard rumours that this is a Hamas reprisal for the killings on the West Bank; but we later learn that it was a simply a fire at an electrical plant. No signs of sabotage.

Our hotel is built into the wall of old Jerusalem, and is pleasingly quaint. "Like something out of a Graham Greene novel," says Richard. Just so: it has long dark corridors, suits of armour, heraldic achievements and ancient weaponry hanging on the walls, as well as oil paintings of assorted holy warriors. There is one portrait of a knight whose beard and slightly pouty expression remind us of the epicene comedian and actor Russell Brand.

Both inside and outside the hotel, we've begun to notice the profusion of the figure known as the Jerusalem Cross, which takes the form of a large central, symmetrical cross – technically known in heraldry as a Cross Potent – with "crossbars" or "crutches" at each point, surrounded by four small crosses. It is supposed to have been derived from the heraldic achievement of Godfrey of Bouillon during the First Crusade; the symbolism of the five crosses is variously said to represent the five wounds of Christ, or Christ flanked by the four Evangelists, or for more arcane meanings. In Old Persian, it signified "Magus". Every pottery in town has

Jerusalem Cross tiles on sale, usually deep red against a cream background.

After dinner, those still lively enough set off in small groups for a night walk through Jerusalem's Old Town – through the souk and down to the Wailing Wall.

The Wall – more than grand and venerable enough to inspire sensations of awe in believers and unbelievers alike – is brilliantly lit by floods, so that in the wide open square before it, anyone with decent eyesight can read a printed text. Which is just what the Orthodox Jewish faithful are doing here – some of them seated at wooden chairs and desks, some of them standing tall, some of them performing to-and-fro movements of sacred ritual. A fascinating sight. Father David, who knows something of the history of Jewish worship, points out to us the details of the dark clothes and headgear of those at prayer – the variations in dress, he tells us, tend to indicate the parts of Europe from which each group came after the founding of Israel.

We walk closer to the Wall – which, we note, is divided into two parts, the left for men, the right for women. We also see an interesting mode of graphic prayer. The faithful write their supplications on small pieces of paper, fold them up and stuff them into cracks between the stones. These days, it is also possible for petitioners far away to send their prayers via email to friends, who then print them out and take them to the Wall.

It is tempting to linger here for hours, but the hour is growing late. As we walk a circuitous route back to the hotel, we can hear, in the distance, what sounds to innocent British ears like a fireworks display. It takes a couple of seconds to make the cultural adjustment, and recognise the noise for what it really is. Machine guns.

Trudie is on mischievous form. In reply to a quiet admonition from Father Richard, she replies "Whatevs, Revs!", then shows us old-timers the insulting gesture known as "Z-Snaps" – you sketch a rapid z-shape in the air with your right hand, snapping the fingers four times to mark the points of the Z. At the same time, you shuffle your head horizontally, like a cobra about to strike.

It is not as easy as it looks.

And so to bed.

DAY SEVEN: SUNDAY 23 MARCH
ST GEORGE'S CATHEDRAL
MUSEUM OF ISRAEL
CHURCH OF THE VISITATION

Communion at St George's Cathedral

Our first full day in Jerusalem begins with a religious service on a grand scale. It is held at St George's Cathedral – more precisely "The Cathedral Church of St

George the Martyr", in East Jerusalem. Founded in 1899, it is also known as "the Mother Church of Anglicanism in the Holy Land", and it sits behind high walls, with a large courtyard. On the church's wall are a number of plaques in English, commemorating the lives and deaths of the British people who served their country in the Holy Land and worshipped here. It is easy to imagine how much it must have prompted nostalgic visions in long-term expatriates.

Father Richard and Father David, looking really rather marvellous this morning in purple stoles, will be among the multi-national group of priests leading this morning's Holy Communion. We feel proud that they are representing us. The local Bishop, whose native language is Arabic but who speaks excellent English, beams widely as he refers to the Rev. Coles as "…our dear Richard!" Richard was here two years ago, and, as so often, has utterly charmed his hosts. Father Richard lowers his eyes, awkward but pleased.

Our Bishop delivers his sermon – first in Arabic, then in English. As far as I can make out from his self-assured body language and the steady, insistent rhythm of his speech, he is an excellent, vigorous preacher in his own tongue. When he repeats the sermon for the benefit of those who do not understand Arabic, it proves to be on the encounter with the Samaritan women. He glosses it very well, finding in it a figure for the process of "discovering the self by discovering

God." It strikes me again how much this mode of explication is like the kind of literary criticism I learned at college.

Astonishingly, there are a few Muslims present at the service as welcome guests. How remarkable to find such an ecumenical spirit in this conflict-ridden city.

As we shuffle out into the brilliant sunlight, a middle-aged woman plays Bach's Toccata and Fugue in D Minor on the organ – not flawlessly, but pretty well. In the courtyard, we sit quietly in the sun and reflect, or talk. Some of our talk is not altogether sacred. There is great mirth at the sight of a foppish young man wearing eye-smackingly bright red trousers – in England, a tribal costume for Hooray Henries. A middle-aged American gentleman called "Bob" takes a keen amorous interest in our Erica, who indulges him for a while before coming back to the safety of a pilgrim huddle. "Was he rich?", Helen asks. Yes, apparently he was very rich. We tease Erica about her forthcoming wedding, and her thousand acre ranches in Texas…

Because it is Mother's Day, we are each presented with a flower, and with small cups of strong coffee.

Another American gentleman, a Pastor who has been working here in the office of Dean for several years, offers to show us round some of the classrooms and visitor accommodation. He is professionally circumspect, but when I quietly ask him whether it isn't difficult being an American in Jerusalem, he admits that he is often pulled into angry conversations with Palestinians who see the USA as their deadly enemy, and with Zionists who feel that the USA is not being a good enough ally. "You know, when you're at home, you feel that it is your right and your duty to complain loudly about all the bad things in America. But when you come to another country, and hear other people running America down... Well…" And he looks rueful. A good man.

Time to move on. Richard is in the best of spirits, full of delight at the incongruous Englishness of this outpost in Jerusalem: "It's as if a little bit of Dorking had been dropped into a land of minarets and lemon trees…"

Partly because we are soon to be gazing on some of the Dead Sea Scrolls, or at any rate some replicas, Father Richard gives us a quick briefing on the Council of Nicæa. This is an immense and complex subject, but, if you were gazing out of the window during Divinity classes, here is a quick summary of Father Richard's talk.

The Council of Nicæa

The Council took place in 325 AD and was commissioned by the Roman Emperor Constantine I, a Christian. Constantine had become troubled by the efflorescence of many incompatible interpretations of scripture – especially the belief known as Arianism – and decided it was time for the representatives of all the churches to gather together and try to thrash out the essentials of Christian doctrine. In other words, it was an attempt to achieve consensus, and considering how difficult it is to bring off that feat at any point in history, it was strikingly successful. High-ranking Church officials came from as far away as Britain – perhaps as many as 1,800 in all, though the figures have been disputed. The Council was called, in Greek, oikumene – strictly "the inhabited earth" or, as we might now put it, "global". Hence the term "ecumenical".

Among its achievements, the Council:

- declared Arianism officially a heresy
- established the date of Easter
- came up with 20 so-called Canon Laws
- and created the first part of the Nicæan Creed.

In effect, it provided the first unified form of Christian doctrine. Though it seems not, despite what the reference books often say, to have decided on the definite contents of the Bible. That process took about another three hundred years. The story is complex, and one of the most dramatic episodes took place only about 70 years ago.

Our next stop:

Museum of Israel: The Model City

Quite a sizeable chunk of the open-air part of the museum is given over to a large-scale model of Old Jerusalem, as it would have been 2,000 years ago. Richard, unimpressed ("It's just a [expletive deleted] model village!"), wanders off to have a cup of tea. But it is good homework for the final stages of our pilgrimage, and Rami gives us a more than usually lively talk as he leads us around. We stroll around the perimeter, as Rami points to the various locations, garnishing the account with some of his inimitable asides and glosses.

— The Temple.
The Holy of Holies.
The Ark of the Covenant... Rami: "In 70 AD, Titus, who was the Roman Commander, destroyed all the Temple, leaving only the Wailing Wall..."

— Temptation Point – "Where the Devil challenged Christ for the third time..."

— The Pool of Bethesda.

— Mount Zion and the place of "Dormition" "Where Mary slept..."

— Three towers from which Herod threw people to their death. "Herod was a Crazy – a killing machine... He killed his two sons by a Jewish wife..."

— The Seven Gates of the city. "One of them is closed…"

— The Wailing Wall "It is the Wall of the Mountain, NOT the Temple…."

— Golgotha "It is BY the city, not IN the city"

As usual, some of his remarks aren't easy to follow, but some of the things he tells us will click into place when we visit the real sites.

Dead Sea Scrolls on Display

After Rami's crash course on the landmarks of Jerusalem, some of us wander downstairs into the cool, dimly lit display of the Dead Sea Scrolls. This domed structure, most of it below the earth, is "Shrine of the Book". The scrolls themselves are too delicate to be suitable for public display, so most of the exhibits on show here are reproductions. No matter: they are exceptionally interesting.

After the Bedouin lads had sold the scraps of leather to the cobbler and part-time antiquities dealer in Bethlehem, Khalil Eskander Shalin – known as Kando, and cousin of those chaps who ran the souvenir shop we visited a few days ago – it took a while for the scrolls to find their way into the hands of scholars, and it wasn't until 1949 that they were traced back to the cave at Qumran. It turned out to have other scraps and evidence that authenticated the scrolls. After that, Bedouin and archæologists were in a race to find more remains in the caves around Qumran. Another ten caves proved to have manuscript remains, most astonishingly cave 4, where 90% of the scrolls were found.

In all 972 manuscript fragments and complete scrolls emerged. Part of the excitement about some of the manuscripts is that they were among the earliest known versions of the Hebrew scriptures; others, more recent – including texts in Aramaic and a few in Greek – greatly augmented our knowledge of non-canonical writings. The conjecture that most of these documents were the work of a group known as the Essenes found swift acceptance, and remained the standard view until the 1990s, when it was seriously challenged, though not entirely refuted.

We know a certain amount about the Essenes from classical writers. In his *Natural History*, Pliny the Elder says that the Essenes did not marry, but lived a communal existence. In *The Jewish War*, Josephus describes them as a minority "philosophical sect", greatly out-numbered by the Pharisees and Sadducees. They followed a much more demanding regime than the other two sects: they kept no slaves, shunned animal sacrifice and could carry weapons only in self-defence. Staring at the scripts from ancient languages induces a state of reverie, but...

"Buddy Call!"

Everyone is a bit tired. Richard joins me at the back of the coach to give a quiet lecture on the transmission of Biblical texts. Once again, I scribble notes which, even a few hours later, prove to be barely intelligible: "Nineteenth Century: the Higher Criticism in Germany.... Erasmus and Origen... Hexapla..."

Oh well. I can look into this later, if need be.

Using the PA, Richard talks to the whole coach about the tradition of burying priests the other way round from the laity. And also about his experiences of seeing monks being laid to rest. "Monks' funerals are lovely. They make you want to die."

Our final stop of the day is also the most beautiful, both in setting and mood.

Village of Ein Karem

This village is believed to be the home of Zechariah and Elizabeth, the parents of John the Baptist, and thus the site (a) of John's birth and (b) of the encounter between Elizabeth and Mary, when the Magnificat was first sung. Many composers, including the greatest, have set the Magnificat, some in Greek or Latin, some in English. The version known to the Anglican church is in the Book of Common Prayer, and begins:

My soul doth magnify the Lord:
  And my spirit hath rejoiced in God my saviour

For He hath regarded:
> The lowliness of his handmaiden

For behold, from henceforth:
> All generations shall call me blessed

For He that is mighty hath magnified me:
> And holy is His name...

There are two main churches in Ein Karem, the Church of St John and the Church of the Visitation – the latter yet another work by Antonio Barluzzi, set on top of a hill, and one of his most pleasing creations. After walking up a fairly steep incline, we hold our evening service. Everyone seems particularly touched by this Evensong. I certainly am. Our walk back down the hill is quiet and thoughtful. The younger and more active take the arms of the older pilgrims, and we make the descent slowly.

✠ ✠ ✠ ✠

Later. Just across from the entrance to the hotel is the Armenian pottery shop mentioned by Father Richard on our first days together. Some of us nip over before dinner to buy their wares, especially images of the Jerusalem Cross and their fine ceramic pomegranates, which range in size from roughly egg-cup dimensions to about the size of a rugby football. Sara is one of the shoppers, and she adds her contribution to the ongoing commentary on pomegranates. Apart from the various

Biblical meanings Richard told us about, the fruit has also, she says, been regarded as a fertility symbol. "Like testicles, they're full of seed…" Trudie points out that when Rami uses the word "pomegranate", it sounds like "hand grenade".

Time for a relaxing pre-dinner drink at the hotel bar. Gins and tonic are the popular choice. For some reason, Bryan and I fall into a discussion about the difference between "tundra" and "taiga". Helen, exaggerating a no-doubt-genuine impatience with this outburst of Typical Male Pedantry, rolls her eyes and mutters imprecations. Nicholas joins us with his latest purchase – a humble wooden cross, which he has had blessed by Father Richard. He explains that his grandmother Hilda, herself a devout Christian, had died just three days before we set off. She was delighted that Nicholas and Colin were making a pilgrimage. Nicholas's plan is to put this small fragment of Jerusalem into Hilda's coffin.

Those of us who went to the Wailing Wall last night comment again on the practice of putting little scraps of paper – written prayers – into cracks in the Wall. For what, we wonder, would people usually pray?

Mo: "Men would pray for more money, women would pray for less sex."

Jerusalem (2)

DAY EIGHT: MONDAY 29 MARCH
HEBRON AND THE TOMB OF THE PATRIARCHS
MOUNT ZION AND THE CENACULUM
DORMITION ABBEY
HOUSE OF CAIAPHAS

The next couple of days will be the most intense of the pilgrimage. They'll include a slow and meditative walk up the Via Dolorosa – the agonising uphill road trodden by Christ on His way to be crucified – and the monastery at Emmaus, where He met with some of His followers soon after the Resurrection.

As we wait for the coach, Nick shows me his iPad, which has Caravaggio's powerful and enigmatic "Supper at Emmaus" (now in the National Gallery, London) as a screen-saver. He tells me that he loved this image well before he found out that many people believe that Caravaggio was what we would now call gay, or about Derek Jarman's film depicting him as a queer hero.

By this stage of the pilgrimage, Nick and Colin

are obviously well-liked by everyone. Some of the pilgrims openly dote on them. Helen:

> "All the women want to take the boys home
> with them"
> Pause.
> "I know I do!"

On the bus, I fall into conversation with Richard.

> Me: "I had strange nightmares last night"
> Richard: "It's because we're getting close to
> Calvary."

It's one of the disconcerting things he says from time to time. Being steeped in secularism, I am usually wrong-footed by these sudden flashes of the largely unfamiliar world inhabited by those with profound faith. Once again, I do a swift inward double-take. Is Richard saying something impish and Wildean? No, I think he means it. He really means it. Though, to be sure, he can also be quite playful about his most treasured beliefs. This morning, a couple of pilgrims have cried off, pleading tiredness. "Those not here today are obviously damned to Hell…." Richard announces, deadpan.

More pop music. Today's earworm is an old disco song from the early 1980s by Mel & Kim: "Respectable", with its annoyingly unforgettable, near-gibberish line "Tay-tay-tay-tay, tay-te-te-te-te-tay tay, Take or leave…" Despite this annoyance, I scribble a memo to myself in my notebook: "I am having a wonderful time."

Rami's talks are becoming more and more politically vehement as we come towards the end of our pilgrimage. He has travelled to Spain and to Mexico, and enjoyed the freedoms he found there. "Here, I am treated as a terrorist!…" Latin America, he believes "is the ideal destination for Christian Palestinians", and he may move there when his children are a little older. Cooling down a little, he describes the various legal anomalies that hang around the rights to old properties.

"If you have documents from the Ottoman period, they can't touch you. But if you have documents that date from the British Mandate, they can do what they like…"

Hebron and the Tomb of the Patriarchs

Hebron, a Palestinian possession, has been hairy for much of the last week, but things seem to have calmed now and we are going to chance it. The last time Richard was here, a couple of years ago, his party was set upon by a gang of angry teenagers who hurled stones at them, and continued hurling stones at their coach as it made a hurried retreat. The approach to the town is not exactly encouraging; as usual, there is a substantial military presence here, watching quietly but obviously on the alert. But today we hardly receive so much as a grim look, and the young Palestinian children who cluster around us as we walk up the slope to the Tomb of the Patriarchs seem happy enough for us to be here, as they pester us for small change or just a little attention.

The Tomb amply repays the mild risk we have taken. Although it is a mosque, and has been so for many years, Christians are welcome to visit provided they follow the decorum. So we remove our shoes, and the women are given headscarves to wear. (Mo comments that the smell is appalling – too many unwashed feet exposed to the air.) Shoes aren't needed, anyway: most of the floors in the rooms and galleries we pass through are covered with fine carpets, in deep shades of red.

Though the main part of the Church was built under the reign of Herod, it was founded on land and over caves which are mentioned in the book of Genesis. Abraham bought the fields as a burial plot, and in the course of time his mortal remains were duly encased here in a cenotaph. It is as the Cenotaph of Abraham that the Tombs are most cherished. In Judaism, it is the second most sacred space on earth after the Temple Mount; and it is just as important in Islam, which regards Abraham as a major prophet. Abraham's son Isaac is also buried here, as are Jacob, Rebecca, Leah and Sarah.

The architecture is well cared-for, and fascinating. The cenotaph of Abraham itself resembles a tall, slender tent with a curved top; its surface is green, decorated with a geometrical pattern of white lines – a tessellation – some of them adorned with diagram-like flower petals. The twin cenotaphs of Isaac and Rebecca are like small, angular houses, with horizontal liver-brown and cream stripes on the walls and all-black roofs. Many of the other details will be familiar to anyone who has ever set foot inside a mosque, such as the prayer niches in the walls. It is a very handsome structure indeed.

Back out into the sunlight, back on to the coach, back past the wary young soldiers and off, with a mild but perceptible sense of relief, for lunch. In need of a spot of frivolity, we talk about light-hearted topics far removed from our surroundings: jazz, Hollywood, Noël Coward…

I have long been itching to tell one of the female pilgrims, Joyce, that she bears a strong resemblance to the great Russian poet, one of my favourites, Anna Akhmatova. This is received with a degree of suspicion until I add the key fact that in her youth Akhmatova was considered one of the great beauties of St Petersburg.

Our next brief visits are all in the vicinity of Mount Zion – just outside the Old City of Jerusalem, near the Zion Gate.

Cenaculum

The "Cenaculum" is believed to be the site of the Last Supper, and thus of the first Communion. As we enter, a minor drama is in progress. A middle-aged man, one of a party of Americans, is rolling on the floor in extreme distress, while paramedics fuss around him and put an oxygen mask on his face. This potential tragedy turns almost at once to farce as his condition is accurately diagnosed as "brain freeze". In other words, he had eaten ice cream too rapidly and given himself a headache. He jumps up as one cured miraculously, and carries on with his friends. Trudie, who has little time for hypochondriacs or softies of any kind, snorts with derision.

Admirers of Leonardo's masterpiece in Milan will probably be disappointed by this room, which is a fairly plain, high space with a vaulted ceiling supported by sturdy stone columns. On the other hand, anyone who imagines the Last Supper taking place in a humble, cosy domestic interior will be quite impressed by the scale of the Cenaculum – grand enough for most mediaeval barons or kings.

Dormition Abbey

Dormition? The phrase is, Father Richard explains, roughly equal to "the Assumption". According to local legend, it is the place where the Blessed Virgin Mary came to die – "sleep" being, then as now, a commonplace euphemism for death. According to Catholic dogma, at the moment of her death she ascended into heaven, body and soul together. Someone ponders what hymn might be appropriate for this site, and a small demon in my brain prompts me to suggest "What Shall We Do With The Drunken Sailor", which has the refrain: "Hooray and Up She Rises"...

I feel duly ashamed of my tasteless gag when I notice a poignant image of the Risen Christ cradling his mother – the opposite arrangement to a standard Pietà. The same image, Richard says, may be found in Hagia Sophia, Istanbul. The existing abbey is fairly modern by the standards of the Holy Land, as it was built at the end of the nineteenth century for a German Benedictine community. The new abbey was erected on the foundations of several previous structures: a Byzantine basilica constructed in the fifth century AD, but destroyed in the Jerusalem siege of 614 AD; and twelfth century abbey of "Our Lady of Mount Zion", duly destroyed in the thirteenth century, at which point the order fled for safety to Sicily. Connoisseurs of hoaxes should note that the French prankster Pierre Plantard deliberately conflated this real-life order with a purely imaginary one when he created the modern myth of the "Priory of Sion" conspiracy, made familiar to millions thanks to that silly novel The Da Vinci Code.

House of Caiaphas

Caiaphas, who is mentioned by Josephus as well as the Gospels, was Christ's worst mortal enemy. It is he who had Jesus brought to trial, convicted, and executed; and Caiaphas was also His gaoler. In the cellars beneath Caiaphas' house lies the pit where Christ was imprisoned on the night before he was brought out for execution. Just a short distance away, Peter was betraying Him thrice. It is a cramped and comfortless deep hole: prisoners would be lowered down into it by ropes, then hoisted up again for their execution. The cellars also contain a crude machine of the kind used to inflict flagellation on the prisoners held here. Salt and vinegar would be rubbed into their open wounds to exacerbate the pain. I am reminded of the punitive cages used as instruments of torture in the middle ages and renaissance – the "Little Ease", in which one can neither stand properly nor sit properly, but only squat in mounting agony. The thought is enough to make me shudder.

We sing a psalm.

And then the Kyrie Eleison.

✠ ✠ ✠ ✠

We end early, at 3.30., because tomorrow will be the most taxing day of the whole trip, both physically and, for those of a spiritual cast, spiritually. Nicholas and a few others head off into the Old Town to buy birthday presents for Richard and JP – there will be a party for them tomorrow night. A few of us cross over the road for al fresco coffee. Mo soon is busy with her knitting needles, making a crocheted garment; Trudie, who takes pride in lacking traditional feminine skills, feigns astonishment at her abilities, and shouts "Spider Mo!" Mo knits on, placidly. Trudie's eyes boggle. "How do you do that? With just a string and a stick!?..."

A local businessmen – a dentist, in fact, of Greek origin (I just about resist the temptation to make a bad pun on the term "Greek extraction") – wanders across to us from his premises just down the street and asks us in good English where we are from. Helen tells him that she is from Yorkshire, which prompts him into floods of reminiscence about the years he spent in the North of England, and his favourite football team, Leeds United.

Richard joins us and tells lots of droll stories from his adventures in Anglicanism. One is about an Archdeacon he knows, who a few years was interrogated quite aggressively when he was trying to pass through Customs at an Australian airport. "Perhaps", the Archdeacon said after a while, "it might speed things up a little if you told me what exactly you are interested in finding?" "Pornography." "Oh, I don't have any of that. I'm afraid I don't even own a pornograph…"

Rested, we wander at a gentle pace down into the

old town, planning to join up with Nicolas and Colin, whom we eventually find at a café, sipping chilled fruit juice and conversing with the establishment's house parrot. Pottery and silverware, mirrors and knives, herbs and spices, fruits and vegetables, fabrics in subtle and gaudy colours, inedible-looking sweets and candies that are still more gaudy, all electric greens, shocking pinks and teal. It is very much like the other souks I have visited – Istanbul, Damascus, Marrakesh – except that that there is less obvious pressure on tourists to stop and buy, less noisy hawking of wares. The proprietor of a handsome antique shop is happy to let us browse and take photographs, proudly showing us an ancient well that goes far down in to the earth. He displays no ill humour when we leave without buying.

Not that the universal habit of pouncing on suckers is absent. I am almost that typical sucker: an importunate stall-keeper asks a fairly whopping 850 shekels for a keffiyeh – the traditional and highly practical Middle Eastern headscarf, at one time common to people of all faiths, but since the 1960s often a signal of Palestinian sympathies. (My desire for one is more adolescent than ideological: I am an incurable T. E. Lawrence bore.) I am about to reach for my wallet when Helen drags me away, tells me I am being ripped off something rotten, and this is so. About 20 yards on, another shop sells me an almost identical scarf for 30 shekels. *Caveat emptor.*

It would be wise to opt for an early bed, and most pilgrims do. But the night is pleasantly warm, and the temptation to sip cold white wine under the stars too powerful for some of us to resist.

DAY NINE: TUESDAY 25 MARCH
BETHANY
MOUNT OF OLIVES
TOMB OF THE PROPHETS
GETHSEMANE AND THE NIGERIANS
POOL OF BETHESDA
VIA DOLOROSA
HOLY SEPULCHRE
ABU GHOSH - EMMAUS

Mount of Olives

And as he sat upon the mount of Olives, the disciples came unto him privately, saying, Tell us, when shall these things be? And what shall be the sign of thy coming, and of the end of the world?
[Matt 24: 3]

According to one tradition, the Mount of Olives is where Jesus taught his disciples the words that we now know as the Lord's Prayer. This doesn't tally with the New Testament account; St Matthew, who gives us the most substantial version of the Prayer, states that Christ taught it immediately after teaching the Beatitudes. Matthew's wording is slightly different from the version I learned as a child. (We used to say "Forgive us our trespasses…")

> After this manner therefore pray ye:
> Our Father which art in heaven,
> Hallowed be thy name.
> Thy kingdom come. Thy will be done
> In earth, as it is in heaven.
> Give us this day our daily bread.
> And forgive us our debts, as we forgive our
>   debtors.
> And lead us not into temptation, but deliver us
>   from evil:
> For thine is the kingdom, and the power, and the
>   glory, for ever.
> Amen.
>
> [Matt. 6: 8-13]

No; according to Matthew, the Mount of Olives was where Christ came immediately before Jerusalem. In defiance of Scripture, the French ecclesiastical body which administers the site celebrates the legend rather than Holy Writ. Plaques on the walls present the Lord's Prayer translated into no fewer than 166 languages: Icelandic, Fijian, Yoruba, French, Kirundi, Tamil….

In the open air, we hold hands in a circle, and say the familiar words together.

On the way out, a merry Arab chap hears us speaking English and teases us: "No fish and chips here!"

The Tomb of the Prophets

A Jewish tradition dating from the middle ages says that somewhere beneath these ruins are buried the three last prophets of the Old Testament: Haggai, Zechariah and Malachi.

This site has by far the most unprepossessing entrance we have so far encountered: a simple block of wood, crudely hand-painted. We descend by tentative steps down into a cave, our way lit only by the small candles each one of us is given to carry. There is, frankly, not much to see here, save for a Greek inscription which, translated, reads:

> Put thy faith in God, Dometila: No human creature is immortal.

Back outside, the sunshine seems brighter than ever, and there is a glorious panoramic view of Old Jerusalem. The golden dome gleams in the distance. I take a photograph of Father Richard and Father David together, smiling, with the vista behind them. Some months later, this very snap ends up in the *Sunday Times* magazine, uncredited, illustrating a feature about Richard.

Rami gives us one of his last lectures – on the theme of Christ's expulsion of the merchants from the Temple, considered from an economic, political and religious point of view. One of his contentions is that Christ was a threat not simply to religious orthodoxy but to the extremely lucrative trade of animal sacrifice. Or, in Rami's words, "The High Priest was getting angry because Jesus touches his pockets."

As so often, it is hard to tell whether Rami's line is strictly orthodox. Still, it is interesting, and I go out of my way to tell him so.

He seems genuinely pleased. "Thank you. So sweet."

Today we will be bumping into other pilgrim bands, most of them European or American and dressed much like us, but our spirits are lifted by a group of Nigerian Christians, the men and women alike dressed in handsome robes of dark green and purple. It makes some of us wonder whether we should not have made a bit more of a sartorial effort.

We take the steep road down towards Gethsemane, some of us quite tentatively. The Nigerians, most of them a fair few years younger than most of us, soon overtake us, half-jogging, half-bouncing, sometimes hand-in-hand, clapping and singing a complex, polyrhythmic African hymn: at once plaintive and uplifting. Beautiful.

I half-seriously propose that it might be a good thing to offer one of our own culture's songs back to them, as a kind of friendly reciprocal gesture, but after a short debate as to what might be suitable –"Don't

Leave Me This Way"? "Jerusalem"? "The Eton Boating Song"? – we admit defeat.

Later, Richard tells me about wonderful sentence he heard from one of our number on the way down: "I tried speaking in tongues once, but all I could come up with was the names of the firemen in Trumpton." For those too young to recall: Trumpton was a sweet-natured animated children's programme from the 1970s. The firemen in question were Pugh, Pugh, Barney McGrew, Cuthbert, Dibble and Grub. Pugh and Pugh were twins.

At the bottom of the road, a local taxi driver looks at the woman standing next to Bryan, and tells him that he is "a lucky man". Unfortunately, the woman is not Mo but Erica. This sets off a lively stream of fantasies about Bryan and Erica running off together….

Gethsemane

Hundreds of pilgrims are here today, and the Church of All Nations – yet another building by Antonio Barluzzi – is so crammed that it is only just about possible to squeeze inside for a quick look at the design. We will hold our small service outside, in a few minutes. The church gardens, full of ancient trees protected from pedestrians by low wire fences, are also crammed. To one side, a film crew are shooting a piece-to-camera. For no reason I can put a finger on, they look German. When I walk past them and eavesdrop, this proves to be the case. What on earth are the tiny signifiers of culture that create this kind of immediate recognition? Beats me.

Because I am by now noted (or, I suspect, privately deplored) for the loudness of my voice, the honour of this reading falls to me. It is from Mark.

> And they came to a place which was named Gethsemane: and he saith to his disciples, Sit ye here, while I shall pray…
>
> [Mark 14.32 and on to 14.42]

Mo proudly tells me that the sheer volume of this reading commands the attention of other groups, who lack a member with a voice suited to the parade ground. Next, we sing the hymn "Praise to the Holiest in the height"… words by the great Roman Catholic writer John Henry Newman. Our Nigerian colleagues look at us with interest. Perhaps we have made the reciprocal gesture after all.

Pool of Bethesda

We know of the pool of Bethesda chiefly from the Gospel according to John, where it is the site of one of Christ's healing miracles.

> Now there is at Jerusalem by the sheep market a pool, which is called in the Hebrew tongue Bethesda, having five porches.

In these lay a great multitude of impotent folk,
of blind, halt, withered, waiting for the moving
of the water...

Thus according to St John (5: 2-3). The apostle
goes on to describe how Jesus miraculously cured a
man who had been afflicted with paralysis for thirty-
eight years.

Jesus saith unto him, Rise, take up thy bed, and
walk.

For centuries, it was assumed that the Pool was
some distance away from Jerusalem, but archæologists
digging here in the nineteenth century uncovered ruins
which suggested that this place, in the part of Jerusalem
now owned by Muslims, was a more likely original.
(Other accounts suggested that the "pool" might only
have been a metaphor.) This theory found strong cor-
roboration as recently as 1964, when further investiga-
tions turned up several layers of sacred buildings,
including Byzantine and Crusader churches, themselves built on top of a temple commissioned by
Hadrian to the Roman gods Æsculapius and Serapis.
So its bona fides are pretty strong.

In the church here we, like most visiting parties,
will again sing a hymn. Immediately ahead of us is a
group of neatly dressed pilgrims from the United States

— at a guess, from a fairly conservative denomination. They have chosen "Amazing Grace", a lovely, heart-piercing song even when artlessly performed. And this is anything but artless. They have arranged it into multiple harmonies, playing to the strengths of their female singers, and it is, simply, gorgeous. We exchange rueful glances. Brian wryly whispers to me, "No pressure, then." Richard quietly suggests to us that the honour of the Church of England is in our hands, or more exactly our throats.

But we are in luck: today's chosen hymn is that marvellous old war-horse "Guide me O thou Great Jehovah", a tune that always makes me think of manly Welsh choirs, and that benefits greatly from what musicologists call "a bit of welly". I am no Pavarotti, nor was meant to be, but when it comes to plain old volume, I'm your man. We pitch in heartily and if the roof is not literally raised, our spirits are. We actually impress ourselves. At the end, Brian warmly shakes my hand. "One-all", he pronounces with satisfaction.

Buddy call.

Via Dolorosa

On the short walk from the car park to the beginning of the Via Dolorosa, Mo stumbles and takes a nasty fall. ("Station three: Christ falls for the first time...") Bryan and I help her to her feet. As we discover later that day, she has broken her rib; but she is determined not to miss the experience, not to make a fuss. This is pluck indeed: Mo finds walking difficult enough at the best of times, and always carries a cane. It seems symbolically apt that at least one of us should make this uphill trek in pain, but I wish it were not dear Mo.

Richard tells us that the busy streets ahead will be crowded and probably at least mildly hostile – "An unfeeling press", as he puts it, with his love of mildly archaic diction. Rami is still gloomier, and warns us that we may well be facing a somewhat dangerous passage. The Via Dolorosa runs through a Muslim neighbourhood, and the locals – understandably – don't always take kindly to Christians wandering through their turf. Much of the Arabic graffiti, he explains, tells Christians exactly what the people of Islam think of them. We may be jeered at, harassed, perhaps even singled out for blows. It is essential that we stick close together and follow his lead.

As it turns out, there is no hostility at all today, and the worst that happens is that the shopkeepers in these narrow alleys try to sell us souvenirs, or entice us into their pizza and kebab joints.

There are fourteen Stations of the Cross.

      1. Jesus is condemned to death.
      2. Jesus receives his cross.
      3. Jesus falls for the first time.
      4. Jesus meets his mother.

5. Simon of Cyrene takes the cross.
6. Veronica wipes the face of Jesus.
7. Jesus falls the second time.
8. The women of Jerusalem weep for Jesus.
9. Jesus falls the third time.

Then:

10. Jesus is stripped of his garments.
11. Jesus is nailed to the cross.
12. Jesus dies on the cross.
13. Jesus is taken down from the cross.
14. Jesus is laid in the tomb.

In churches around the world, congregations have been acting out a metaphorical progress through the Stations since the fifth century or even earlier, but the walking of the Via Dolorosa itself only became a practice after 1342, when the Franciscans were given authority over the Christian holy places in Jerusalem. It was the Franciscans who drew up the list of fourteen stops, and who identified the parts of the Way where the events on the walk to crucifixion took place.

This afternoon will stop at each of these fourteen stages, and try to contemplate the significance of each Station. Richard and David and Sarah, three of the most High Church of those among us, all kneel at the start of each Station. Mo and Bryan, both Catholics, do not. Then we all join together with a short and simple chant:

Jesus, remember me, when You come to Your Kingdom.

Richard explains to us that the first nine Stations at which we will pause are recognised as such more on the grounds of Franciscan tradition than of unambiguous historical evidence. The last five, close to and within the Church itself, are, as he puts it, "confirmed".

It is very difficult to keep the ritual nature and the significance in mind as we pass through the busy crowds and the shouts of stall-holders; the bustle of the marketplace never lets up. Nor do bodily temptations. Nicholas, feeling peckish, buys a chocolate bar and grins like a cheeky schoolboy as he tucks into it. Still, somehow or other we manage to maintain an appropriate solemnity.

After the first seven stations, Richard suggests that we pause to answer our more humble bodily needs: "This sounds very Church of England, but there is time now for a pee and a tea…" So we take up his offer. And then we carry on through the crowds and the bustle until we reach:

The Church of the Holy Sepulchre

Rami offers us a few key moments of the Church's history. The first structures here were said to have been commissioned by Hadrian, who had a Temple of Venus built over Calvary/Golgotha, no doubt as of way of deterring early Christians from making the area a place of homage. An invasion in the year 614 by the Sasanian Empire destroyed all the Christian churches in or near Jerusalem, and much of the existing structure was built by Crusaders. Some of the columns in the courtyard are marked with Crusader graffiti – crosses. The Church belongs to the Greek Orthodox Patriarch and other Christian denominations; there is no permanent presence here of Anglican or other Protestant faiths.

Father Richard adds a curious fact: nowadays, two Muslim families look after the Gate into the Church. There were originally two main entrances, identical arches, but the one to the right has been bricked up. I notice a strange decoration on the outer wall which looks very much like the Norse rune "algiz". Did the Vikings make it as far east as Jerusalem?

The interior overwhelms several senses at once. The eye: the scale of the interior is enormous, and on all sides there are vast mosaics, rocks, shrines. The ear: hundreds, maybe thousands of loud pilgrim voices, and the thunderous music of the organs. The nose: thick incense and sweat. We are jostled, and try hard to stick together in the milling crowd. Rami has warned us that the friction between the supposedly harmonious groups of Christians can result in angry arguments and sometimes even fist-fights. No sign of violence today, but it's not easy to shuffle around without banging into others. For the first time ever, we see Rami high-fiving and joshing with one of the uniformed guards here – obviously an old buddy.

To the south of the main altar is a stairway leading up to the exact spot where Christ was crucified. This afternoon it is so crammed that there is no chance to climb it. Instead, we gather immediately beneath it. For the one and only time on this pilgrimage, I have a bewildering sense of the true strangeness of visiting a shrine.

I am standing under Golgotha.

Under the place where Christ was killed.

The sense of discombobulation lasts for the rest of the visit. I am in a mild daze as we gaze at Christ's tomb, at the Stone where Joseph of Arimathea anointed Christ's corpse…

Whereof we cannot speak, thereof we must be silent.

✠ ✠ ✠ ✠

We take lunch a couple of hours than usual. It is time for us to bid farewell to Rami. We sing "For he's a jolly good fellow!" and Father Richard discreetly slips him a generous tip. He grins and shakes hands and generally behaves as if we have been a lovely audience and a joy to accompany. I realise I will miss his quirky commentaries, rants and all.

As the others drink coffee and chat, I sit alone at a table and spend a few agreeable minutes writing a light acrostic poem for Richard's birthday celebrations tonight.

Abu Ghosh, also known as Emmaus

Rush hour traffic out of Jerusalem is dense, indeed so dense that we are sometimes brought to a complete halt. I fall into discussion with Brian, a witty fellow who writes the Finedon pantomime every year. The puns are dreadful.

Our final destination for the day, and for the whole Pilgrimage, will be Emmaus.

Let Father Richard cite the text, and gloss it.

… just after the events of Easter, two disciples are walking to a village outside Jerusalem and are joined by a stranger on the way who seems not to have heard of the momentous events that have happened in the city. As they walk on he interprets the Bible to them, and they are so captivated by him that when they arrive at Emmaus, even though he wants to walk on, they ask him to stay the night.

When he was at table with them, he took bread, blessed and broke it, then gave it to them. Then their eyes were opened, and they recognised him; and he vanished from their sight. They said to each other: "Were not our hearts burning within us while he was talking with us on the road, while he was opening the scripture to us?"

Then they got up and returned to Jerusalem; and they found the eleven and their companions gathered together. They were saying: "The Lord has risen indeed, and he has appeared to Simon!"

Then they told what had happened on the road, and how he had been made known to them in the breaking of the bread.

Jesus comes to them while they walk and talk, reveals who he is at dinner, and disappears.

Richard's punch-line gives me a chill:

"It is this passage of scripture that made me a Christian."

We arrive almost an hour later than intended. The door of Emmaus is closed, and there does not seem to be anyone in the grounds, but finally one of the Brothers – this is a French Benedictine order – spots us through a fence and unbolts the door. Our two fathers join him for a quick conference.

Helen immediately sees the resemblance here to the standard confrontation with a bouncer outside a night club. "Yer name's not on the list, yer not coomin' in…" But the Brother is no petty-minded jobsworth; on the contrary, he greets us kindly and cheerily and lets us in to enjoy the garden while he goes to confer with his superiors. The garden is indeed something to enjoy – a hortus conclusus, a little island of greenery and calm kept safely behind walls. There are tall trees and lush grass, and it is all surprisingly quiet even though the main road is just yards away.

I find myself standing next to Joyce, and tell her an anecdote about a Catholic friend of mine, a mediaevalist, who a few years ago was in the gift shop at Ely Cathedral and decided to buy a crucifix on a silver necklace for his god-daughter.

"Good afternoon. I'd like to buy a crucifix, please."

"Certainly, Sir. What kind would you like?"

"Which kinds are there?"

"Well, two really. One is just a plain old cross, and one has a little man on it…"

Joyce laughs, and shows me the crucifix hanging from her own neck. It is plain. "We don't have the body of Christ on our crosses, because He was resurrected…" I am ashamed not to have known this fact.

Twenty minutes or so pass, and our smiling host comes back to us with, so to say, his blessing. (Later, Father Richard explains to us that the Benedictines are noted for their principle of hospitality to strangers.) It will be quite all right for us to hold our mass in an hour or so; meanwhile, would we care to attend the

order's Solemn Vespers? We most certainly would, and
we do not regret it.

The chapel is sparely decorated, finely propor-
tioned, gracefully and cunningly lit. On the Eastern
wall is a badly damaged fresco; otherwise there is little
in the way of decoration save for candles and altar
cloth. As we wait for the Benedictines to file in, I re-
mark to Richard that I think my eyeballs must in some
way be Protestant. It's exactly the Protestant plainness
and lack of fleshly imagery that makes this Catholic
space so spiritually intense, even for an unbeliever.

When the Solemn Vespers begins, there is a simi-
larly austere elegance and beauty in the sounds and
gentle bodily motions of these acts of worship. In the
body of the chapel sit about some thirty monks and
nuns, who sing to the musical accompaniment of a
keyboard that looks something like a giant harpsichord.
Today is the Feast of the Annunciation, so the elderly
Abbot is presiding, sparely splendid, holding a crosier.
He gives the reading in melodious French: it is a passage from Revelation, "Lo, I beheld a new heaven and
a new earth..." We British pilgrims sit behind the
Benedictines, standing when appropriate, joined by a
handful of young French Catholics, mainly girls.

As someone who has little experience of such mys-
teries, I do not notice that there is anything unconven-
tional about their acts of worship. Later, Trudie explains to me how unusual the singing was: "Normally, a

Vespers would have a set pattern to it. But this was petitioning by notes in prayer. They weren't actually saying anything but free-styling it as it were. So one nun/monk would sing some notes to God and then another would follow with their notes. Each seemed to know when the other had finished. None of them interrupted but just seemed to pick up where the other left off…"

When our hosts are done, Richard passes out the order of service – because we are running late, we will leave out a couple of hymns and a couple of readings. Richard improvises an excellent sermon, taking as his text the severely damaged fresco of the Crucifixion. The central figure of Christ has been erased by time, leaving the most vivid figures the disciples and family of Jesus: people without real power, middling people, neither rich nor poor: people just like us.

The most distinct figure is that of the Thief who was Saved. Richard has forgotten his name, and to my surprise as much as anybody's, I fetch it up from my memory: Dismas. (Many years ago, I had some dealings with a place called Dismas House, in Nashville, a church-funded hostel for ex-convicts looking to go straight.) Father Richard elaborates on the significance of the Saved Thief. A reminder, as Samuel Beckett famously observed, that even the worst of sinners need not necessarily despair of their future state. A few hours later, Richard consults his books or his phone and discovers that today is also St Dismas's Day.

It is time for the Sign of Peace. Everyone is aware that this will be our last service together, and the wistfulness that comes over every group that has shared a brief time together is magnified by the spiritual context. With those I don't know too well, I make sure to shake their hand firmly, smile warmly and look directly into their eyes, affirming that I am not the outsider I was nine days ago. With those who have grown to be new friends, I develop the handshake into a hug. Nicholas, whether he likes it or not, receives a manly kiss on the cheek.

Outside it is dusk. We linger just a few minutes to enjoy the night air and the scent of flowers, and to digest the emotions a little. But there's no time to be too melancholy: tonight we have birthdays to celebrate.

Birthday Jollities

Back at the hotel, washed and brushed up and with a couple of aperitifs under the belt, we gather for dinner and jollities.

Brian does the warm-up act, drawing heavily on Finedon pantomimes of recent years. Audience participation is lively:

> "Oh no it isn't!"
> "Oh yes it is!!"

Do any nations other than the United Kingdom

go in for our kind of pantomime rituals? I somehow
doubt it. Next, Brian introduces me and my birthday
acrostic. "Audrey", you may recall, is one of Richard's
sweet young dachshunds.

> Reverend Coles, you Prince of Vicars,
> In whom the lamp of Wisdom flickers,
> Communard back in the Eighties,
> Highbrow judge of matters weighty,
> Audrey's favourite human pet,
> Raconteur… Let's not forget
> Distinguished scholar of True Writ,
> Connoisseur, savant and wit,
> Or simply this: a Diamond Bloke.
> Let me just say – and it's no joke –
> Each one of us thinks that you're great.
> So have a Happy Birthday, mate!!

Needless to say, several pilgrims complain that I
should have rhymed "vicars" with "knickers".

The lights suddenly cut out and the room is filled
with an alarming uproar of yowling, banging, and clat-
tering. A terrorist attack? No, nothing more sinister
than the restaurant staff, wheeling in a trolley with a
great big cake for the birthday boys, ablaze with
candles. Cheers and the traditional singing of the
Happy Birthday song.

Richard, making no attempt to hide his delight at
being the centre of attention and affection, poses for a

dozen or more cameras wearing his new fez, while JP stands grinning next to him, sporting his new keffiyeh.

✠ ✠ ✠ ✠

About half an hour later, both Richard and I take a break from the party and sit down in quiet for a few minutes in the hallway. I thank Richard for the experiences of the past ten days, and try to explain how it has affected me – not an easy task, as I am not sure how to summarise such a tangle of impressions and experiences. I muse that it would make a wonderful end to this narrative if I were able to declare myself a convert. Sadly, I can't; not in any unequivocal way, at least.

"No, of course not," says Richard, reassuring as ever. "That would have been tacky."

And yet I do feel that something about this experience has got under my skin – not anything directly religious, perhaps, but a sense of pleasure in having been accepted so warmly and unhesitatingly by a group of strangers. As someone who spends most days entirely alone reading or scribbling, and on the whole enjoys the solitary life of the full-time writer, it has been unexpectedly refreshing to feel part of a team again...

Richard goes back to the party, and I sit on my own for a while, thinking about the sermon Trudie gave about the miracle of the Transfiguration. Like Trudie's conversational style, it was a strange mixture of comedy and profundity. She started by saying "I always feel sorry for the apostles who didn't get chosen. I mean, why those three? If you are going to perform this miracle, why not show everyone?..."

She concluded: "It's as if the Transfiguration is the thing they've been waiting for, it's arrived, job done... For me that's what this trip is like, I've seen the sights, job done, and yet of course there is sooooooo much more. Not only in terms of more to see, but like the gospel itself one suspects that the real work will only be done after the trip, on our return, in our interaction with others."

Amen.

First edition published by Kindle Editions

First paper edition published 2016 by
Pallas Athene (Publishers) Ltd
Studio 11B
Archway Studios
25-27 Bickerton Road
London N19 5JT

ISBN 978 1 84368 143 4

Layout and typesetting
Alexander Fyjis-Walker, Patrick Davies and Anaïs Métais

www.pallasathene.co.uk
Twitter: @Pallas_books
Facebook: @pallasathenebooks

Printed in England